Traveling in Style

Part 1: Three Years of RV Camping

Part 2: Nine Years of RV Living

Traveling in Style

    Part 1, Three Years of RV Camping

    Part 2, Nine Years of RV Living

Copyright © 2015 by Edward Dingledy

Cover photograph: Steve Pedersen

Proof readers: Bob Barker, Betsy Dingledy

Contents

Preface 5

Introduction 6

PART 1   THREE YEARS OF RV CAMPING   9

Chapter 1 First Trip, Alaska 9

Chapter 2 Texas 16

Chapter 3 Eastern Canada 28

Chapter 4 Great Lakes 35

Chapter 5 Cross Country 1 44

Chapter 6 Cross Country 2 62

PART 2   NINE YEARS OF RV LIVING   77

Chapter 7 Full Timing 77

Chapter 8 California, Oregon 81

Chapter 9 Western Canada 88

Chapter 10 Rocky Mountains 100

C hapter 11 Southwest 112

Chapter 12 Glacier NP Volunteers 119

Chapter 13 Shenandoah NP 136

Chapter 14 Final Trip 143

Preface

This is a story, not a travel log, about travel and some of the places we visited during our RV experience. It was frequently educational, sometimes exciting and always entertaining. The places described here are just a few of the places we visited. They are the ones that we particularly enjoyed. Some have historical significance or great scenery. Others included special golf courses, beautiful gardens, and great hiking trails. In addition, the RV gave us the opportunity to visit family and longtime friends we hadn't seen in many years.

Part 1 describes our early RV camping experiences which were based on three month winter escape trips and shorter summer camping trips. It is based on our original RV premise that where ever you live, for three months of the year, you'd rather be somewhere else.

Part 2 describes our full time RV living experience and the benefits of extended stays in various regions. It greatly expanded our original premise. We got to experience new places, made new friends and built new long term lasting relationships.

Introduction

The trailer was packed and we were ready to leave. We closed the door to the house for the last time, gave the keys to the RE agent, got into the car, started out the driveway when the back door of the trailer opened, dropped to the ground, and cargo spilled out. An inauspicious beginning to our great adventure, living full time in an RV.

The decision on this adventure reflected our desire for something new. Our country is unique in its size, infrastructure, scenery, parks, historical sites, and diversity and one of the most efficient and enjoyable ways to visit these sites is in an RV. You can travel all around the country in comfort or stay in one place for an extended period with the flexibility to try different areas.

There is no packing and unpacking, no problem forgetting something at home, no problem taking pets. Traveling to a warmer climate in the winter and taking our hotel room with us, along with a kitchen and bathroom is pretty efficient, reducing the need for hotel reservations.

Communication technology has made RV travel much easier. When we started in 2001, high speed internet was available but it required access to a hot spot, something not every RV Park had. Nor was every RV equipped with an antenna for satellite TV. Email was still somewhat new and few banks had electronic banking. That has all changed. The air card provides high speed internet via cellular towers and opens up high speed communication for email and electronic banking. Satellite TV means that your RV can be in the middle of the desert and you can still see the Super bowl on HD TV. Maps are great, but a GPS makes it even easier. But, they do make mistakes so maps are still important.

All of this technology is continuing to evolve. Forwarding mail, paying bills, and accessing information is getting even easier and is no longer a barrier to managing one's affairs while traveling.

RVs come in many sizes and prices. Small RV's (24' – 30') are perfect for weekend camping or vacation travel. Living in one full time is more comfortable in a larger RV. But the fun and travel opportunities are common to both.

There is a reason so much of the world wants to come here as tourists. With our roads, RV parks, and support facilities throughout the country, we have the infrastructure in place to offer a truly great travel experience. And the people you meet along the way – priceless!

Part 1   Three Years of RV Camping

Chapter 1 First Trip, Alaska

It seemed like the stars all lined up for us.

In the summer of 2001, I was reading a self-published RV book from Amazon about interesting RV trips. One of them was intriguing because it included a rental RV for a one-way trip from Seattle to Alaska, dropping off the RV in Anchorage and taking a cruise on the inland waterway back to Vancouver, BC. After a couple of nights in Vancouver the final leg was a train trip from Vancouver to Seattle. I had always wanted to travel the country in an RV. Betsy, on the other hand, was not very enthusiastic about the RV, but always wanted to visit Alaska. Our oldest daughter lived in Seattle. It would be an opportunity to visit with her and see her new home. There was also an extended family reunion in Tahoe, CA, starting on Sept 15, 2001. Everything fit together. We booked the trip and flew from Connecticut to Seattle in mid-August.

The rented RV was a 25' cab over 'class C' RV. This is an RV that looks like a truck with a camper on the truck bed and a sleeper compartment with window over the cab. A perfect size particularly for first time users and for weekend trips. It is easy to drive, easy to park and fairly inexpensive to operate. Our rental was basic, with few bells and whistles which meant less to learn and still have the features needed to live in for the two week trip from Seattle to Anchorage by way of Fairbanks and Denali. The rental company had made all the arrangements for the trip. The route was laid out, campgrounds prearranged and fees paid, train reservations to Seward and cruise tickets all included.

After learning the basics about the RV, light switches, valves, levers, knobs, filling water tanks etc., we had a session of emptying the grey water (liquid waste) and black water (solid waste) tanks. It was a lot easier than expected which relieved all our anxieties about that operation. Then we hit the road!

We were late arriving at the first campground and it was dark and closed. Common sense usually prevails and there was a bulletin board with our name, site number and a campground map showing the location of the site. Hooking up in the dark was pretty easy – plug into the electrical post and connect a hose. We passed our first test.

In the morning, we learned one of the first unwritten RV travel rules: get to the campground early. The early arrivals were parked with the water view, looking out to the San Juan Islands. We, being the last arrivers, were facing (and smelling) the bog. Not much of an incentive to stick around so we decided to get started and cross into Canada before the border crossing got too crowded. How naïve … it is always crowded.

Our first travel day going through British Columbia set the tone for a wonderful RV experience. It is beautiful. Most of the trip was highways travel which obviously is much easier than local streets and a good way to acclimate to driving an RV rather than a car. British Columbia has wonderful gardens viewable from the road which makes the drive so pleasant and relaxing. The environment of mild wet winters, with sunny but cool summers is a perfect combination for manmade landscaping. Nature's landscaping with the mountains, trees and water is equally spectacular. Driving the Alaska (Alcan) Highway is one of the great and most popular RV trips for good reason.

The drive to Fairbanks took a leisurely seven days, going through Prince George, Dawson Creek (mile 0 of the Alaskan Highway), Fort Nelson and Whitehorse. Then into Alaska. About 190 miles north of Fort Nelson, near milepost 499 is Laird Hot Springs. That is a nice stopping point. After parking the coach, we got into our bathing suits, took the boardwalk to the hot springs, jumped in the springs and relaxed. Occasionally there are bears on the boardwalk and they also like to relax in the hot springs. It is best to let them go first.

There are other stops along the way for lunch or a picnic but there is no reason to hurry. We only stopped when we wanted to, since with a motor coach there is no need for pit stops, since the pit is in the coach.

We spent a few days in Fairbanks and, when our Seattle daughter heard we were having such a good time, she flew up to Fairbanks to join us. Now we had 3 adults in a 25' RV. No problem except that I was assigned to the sleeping compartment bed over the cab. Usually that is for the kids, but, other than occasional night time trips to the bathroom, it worked. I stepped on Betsy's head only once getting down. We were fortunate in that the northern lights were on display one of the nights in Fairbanks.

We met two couples from North Carolina who were packed into a 22' rental RV. Close quarters, but they were having a great time, sampling the beers from all the Alaskan breweries. They pointed out they were professional beer drinkers and were not affected as much as amateurs would be. In the morning, they were on their way and looking forward to getting to Anchorage for a new round of local pubs to visit.

We spent 3 days in Denali and took a bus trip into a remote campsite site past Denali (formerly Mt McKinley) within the park. There was a flight available for hire to fly around the mountain for the return to the RV campground. Our daughter, a mountain climber, took the flight and put Denali on her bucket list of mountains to climb. We met a couple from Utah who raised various types of garlic and they and Betsy discussed which to use with which foods. When we got back to Connecticut, there was a package waiting for us with various kinds of garlic from Utah.

On the way to Anchorage, we passed through Palmer and, being the end of summer, the Alaska State Fair was open. State Fairs are pretty much the same throughout the country, but with some regional features. The Alaska Fair has something shared by no other region, the giant vegetables. Alaska has a short growing season but a long growing day, up to 24 hours for most of the summer. There are various theories such as the soil, fertilizer, personal care and seeds, and I am sure all were factors, but the one thing that is unique to Alaska is the length of the daylight sun, so I am going with that as the main factor. Regardless of the reason, the large vegetable competition is fierce and to see beans over 30 inches long, pumpkins over 1000 lbs., huge zucchinis and squash, the Alaska State Fair in Palmer is your only choice.

Eklutna Alaska is on the northern side of Anchorage and on the way from Palmer. It was settled by Russian Orthodox Missionaries in 1840 and their influence is seen today particularly by the graves which are covered with brightly painted spirit houses. When I first saw them in the early 60's during my 2-year Army career, they were in disrepair but they are now well maintained and are quite an interesting cultural icon.

Our RV trip came to an end in Anchorage, our last night in the RV. The next morning, we took a scenic train trip to Seward to the ship for our cruise down the inland water away to Vancouver, BC. After a couple of days in Vancouver we took the train back to Seattle, arriving on the night of Sept 10, 2001 and made our plans for the drive to the Tahoe family reunion.

The 9/11 attacks the next morning changed many of our plans. We were the only east coast relatives who got to a rather subdued reunion.

The fun we had in the RV set the tone. The events of 9/11 made the decision inevitable. We canceled any plans for foreign travel and decided to buy an RV instead and visit places in our country.

Chapter 2 Texas

We became the proud owners of a 2-year-old used 36' Winnebago Adventure Class A gas driven motor home. RVs are good for domestic camping as well as travel camping. When not in traveling use, the young neighborhood girls used it for tea parties. We also took advantage of our portable guest quarter on certain occasions. Our family has an annual Thanksgiving family reunion and the hosting responsibility rotates among Ed and his sisters. It was our turn to host this year so we turned the house over to my sisters, daughters, and brothers in law, while Betsy and I slept peacefully in the RV.

Our initial experience in an RV was a 25' camper. Now we were driving a 36' bus. As the salesman told us as we took our first drive around the block, 'don't worry about the other drivers, let then worry about you, - you are much larger'. Most RV'ers pull a car for local travel. We chose to get a carrying platform for a Honda Helix motor scooter rather than tow a car. Both of us were comfortable using motorcycles and it made backing up the RV a lot easier.

An advantage of traveling in an RV is that there is no need to kennel your pets when traveling - the dogs come with us. We had two fairly large dogs, Chilly, a yellow lab female and Max, an Irish setter male and they loved to travel. Max, in particular, liked to sit on the passenger seat and, if Betsy did not move, he would climb on her lap. Max weighs about 90 lbs., a bit large for a lap dog. He eventually pushed Betsy to the couch and he took over the seat himself. With his red fur, it looked like I had a red headed wife riding with me who looked like a dog.

No matter how thoroughly one plans the first trip some things will be overlooked. We were about four hours late in getting on the road because even though there was no snow on the ground, the air was cold and water freezes. The water was hooked up for Thanksgiving and it wasn't disconnected from the RV after the weekend. We had to wait for the hose to thaw to fill the water tank.

We scouted the campgrounds and found one that remained open all year and it was within our driving distance, so we headed out. Because of our late start, we did not get to the campground until after dark. We did not know the area, so finding the campground was a bit tricky. The entrance had two accesses, one coming from the north and the other coming from the south. We made the mistake of thinking one was the entrance and the other was the exit. So I tried the second entrance. Wrong! We got hung up and stopped traffic until we got untangled. We did learn a good lesson as well; most RV'ers are very patient and considerate of rookie RV'ers.

Texas seemed like a fun place to start. This was another trip mentioned in the RV travel book and made sense to us because it would be warmer and inexpensive with wide open roads. In addition, my roommate when I first lived in New York was from Abilene, Texas. He always had some unique Texas comments. Once when I was concerned about something very minor. He set me straight when he told me that I looked more nervous than a blind queer at a wienie roost. Great comment 40 years ago before present day political correctness.

Our first stop was New Orleans. Because of the tragedy of 9/11, the Super Bowl scheduled for the Super Dome in New Orleans was moved back a week. That in turn, changed the first parade of Mardi Gras which gave us an opportunity we had not anticipated

The parades provide the entertainment, but the crowds provide most of the fun. A drunk guy near us held up pair of panties, yelling at attractive girl on float, 'Hey sweetie, did you leave these in my room last night?' She probably has heard that before, because she didn't miss a beat, 'No, but don't you wish I had.' However, the floats, bands and costumes were up to PG standards.

We spent a couple of days in New Orleans then headed out to our next stop, San Antonio, TX.

Of all the places in Texas, the Hill country in Texas, is one of the most attractive. San Antonio and Austin, the state capital have style and a personality. The river walk in San Antonio is one of the most popular tourist attractions in Texas and one of the most attractive places anywhere in the country. It is a public park with a network of walkways along the river, one story below street level. The walkways are lined with restaurants, bars, and shops on both sides of the river beautifully landscaped with gardens, fountains and waterfalls. It is alive with activity and musical events. It was conceived in the late

1920's for flood control but community leaders had the vision to see the commercial and tourist potential and in 1938, got approval and broke ground in 1939. It has continued to expand and is a relaxing way to spend the evening walking along the walkway, stopping for cocktails or a meal at an outdoor café.

The LBJ Homestead and Library in Johnson City reflects his personality and presidential style. It is one of the northern points of a triangle with Austin 60 miles due east and San Antonio 70 miles due south. They are all within an hour or so drive from each other and since this is considered the prettiest part of Texas, see them all. It is such a small part of Texas; you can't afford to miss visiting any of this area. After this, it is a long drive to west Texas.

Fredericksburg nearby is a German style small town just west of the Johnson Ranch that has great German food. Nearby is Kerrville where there is a very attractive RV park combined with small houses and a popular retirement community for RV'ers.

After the hill country, it is rather sparse driving to Fort Stockton then down to Big Bend NP, one of the more remote and least known and visited NP. It is too bad because it is a wonderful Park. It is on the border with Mexico where the Rio Grande bends north and is quite different the geography normally associated with Texas. It has as much New England topography as Mexican and the climate has a similar contrast, in the mountains, it is cool and the flat area, it is hot.

While driving around on our motor scooter, we stopped by the visitor's center. There was a great relief map of the park. We were studying it and somebody said something that made Betsy laugh. A lady liked her laugh because, as she described it, it was a happy laugh. She invited us to join them for their Pioneer Reunion, an annual event where the descendants of the original settlers, some from 1840 gathered around and repeated stories they heard from their parents and grandparents about life during pioneer times. The stories were a perfect example of the oral tradition. The stories were the history of that time – before radio, TV and, obviously, the internet. The stories included Comanche and Apache Indian raids, getting mail and grocery shopping by horseback 100 miles away once a month, and picking up a skunk that got into a house by the tail so it could not spray. We never got the last part of that story, i.e., how did they release it without getting sprayed. A lot of the stories were about local people who were interesting to the pioneer descendants but there were so many that were just funny and interesting without the need to know the people involved. It was a fascinating few hours with some really interesting and typically Texas story telling.

Big Bend in February has beautiful weather. It just didn't seem like winter. Canoeing on the Rio Grande seemed like a good summertime activity that we could enjoy in the winter. We rented a canoe with the guide that came with it and had a nice leisurely paddle on calm waters through the canyons. Then we came to some fairly, I assumed, mild rapids. The guide suggested it might be wise to wade through the rapids and pull the canoe because of the strong undertow. Having canoed in rivers and streams in New England, mild rapids are not a problem. No reason for us to walk through the rapids. Big mistake. The undertow is stronger than we anticipated and we got dumped twice into the Rio Grande. In February the air, particularly in the sun is nice and warm, but the water in the Rio Grande comes from the mountains in the north and, and in the shade of the canyon walls, it was cold. Misplaced arrogance can be penalized by nature. We listened to guide the rest of the trip.

In 2002, one could cross the Rio Grande into Mexico with no problems. The traffic went both ways, to the extent that the Mexican kids on the border, with mutual agreement by families on both sides of the border, crossed over every day to go to school in Texas. And, for tourists and Texas natives there was a small rowboat/ferry that took us over to Mexico where there were burros waiting to take us up about a mile to a taco stand. Three tacos and a beer for $1 and it is real Mexican. The meat probably was goat, but it could have been something else and we would have no idea. For $2, it was a nice meal, with liquid refreshment and a fun experience. It is a shame that the border is now closed so that experience is no longer available.

After a week in Big Bend it was time for the next stop, Fort Davis. We toured the frontier fort, now part of the National Park Service. It is one of the last and best of the remaining frontier forts built during the Indian Wars and was one of the home forts for the 'Buffalo Soldiers' who distinguished themselves in battles with the Apaches and Comanche. MacDonald Observatory is close by and available for visits and 'Star Parties' at night. The observatory is well situated in the mountains with a very dark nighttime sky, one of the darkest in the lower 48 states which makes it perfect for star gazing.

The little town of Marfa is also near. That is the location where *Giant* was filmed in the late 1950's. If you visit, you can only imagine the excitement this little town on West Texas had when Elizabeth Taylor, Rock Hudson and James Dean moved there for months during the filming. Another place where a movie was filmed was Brackettville, TX on Route 90 off Route 277 heading toward McAllen. That is where John Wayne built a reduced size replica of the Alamo for his 1960 movie *The Alamo*. The set was used for a number of other western movies and TV programs, including *Gunsmoke* .We decided to be real tourists and watch them make a movie and see the set. There was a large field where coaches could park. So we left the dogs in the coach, opened some windows and went to watch the making of a movie. Obviously, it was a western, and there were cattle being led to the set through the coach parking area. The dogs noticed them and did not like it. There also was a gun battle and the dog liked that even less. When we got back to the coach, their response was quite evident because they tore up the inside of the coach. Nothing that could not be fixed, or, in a number of areas, replaced. But, it was an expensive attraction.

We then went down to McAllen and Donna, on the southern Texas border sometimes referred to as the 'Texas Riviera'. Both towns are close to the Mexican border and we could drive there in about 15 minutes, get a $3 haircut, $3 meal and $3 bottle of decent (aged 36 months) Scotch Whiskey and cross back to the US for cocktails. We have not been back there for 12 years and probably much has changed. More security at the border and, with the new prosperity in Mexico, the prices undoubtedly have changed, but the friendliness and local charm I suspect, remain the same.

After a week or so, it was time to move on – next stop, Corpus Christi, about 2 ½ hours north. It was their annual oyster festival weekend, and Betsy loves oysters, so we got on the scooter and drove from our campground on the highway about 10 miles to the festival on the docks. It didn't seem like it would be a problem. In mid-march on the Gulf Coast, we assumed it would be cool, but not cold. We were wrong - it was cold, about 35 degrees. The oysters were great 10 for $5.00, but the drive to and from the festival gave us our first hint that we needed something else to use for local transportation. That scooter ride was so cold, it took us a day and night to thaw out. More lessons occurred before we finally broke down and decided to tow a car.

We enjoy visiting gardens and the south in the spring is the place to be. We took a leisurely 2 day drive to Theodore Alabama, just south of Mobile to see the Bellingrath Gardens, 65-acre garden and grand estate home of Walter and Bessie Bellingrath. He was a successful businessman – he got one of the early distribution Coca Cola franchises. The gardens and house are a testament to his and Coca Cola's early and ongoing success. All of the gardens are a treat, but if you get there in the early spring, the azaleas around Mirror Pond is a view one will never forget. We spent an entire day strolling the grounds visiting all the various gardens and finding a time and place for picnic lunch. It was a wonderful day. Interestingly, we did not know anything about the gardens and were told about them by some RV'ers we met along our travels. We learned a lot from people we met along the way.

It was getting close to April and we had our 3 months on the road. The snow is gone back home and the grounds needed cleaning up, lawn fertilized, grass mowed, bushes pruned, and all the other chores that had been neglected while traveling. We are home for the season… but not quite. Eastern Canada beckoned.

CHAPTER 3 EASTERN CANADA

When it gets hot and sticky in Connecticut, it is time to go north. Fifteen daughters, cousins, siblings nieces and nephews were camping in Acadia National Park in Maine for the July 4th weekend and the RV was perfect for our type of camping – electricity and hot water even though the campground had no hookups. Generators are fine during daytime and our water tanks were full. We became the gathering place for the older generation at night. Campfires are for the younger generation.

Since we were close to Nova Scotia, we just continued on to the St John/Digby Ferry from New Brunswick to Nova Scotia. The cost of the ferry was about the same as cost of the gas in Canada, and this was a pleasant change. Digby on Nova Scotia is known for its scallops. After all the lobster and shrimp in Maine, scallops sounded good (even if it was just a variation of the shell fish menu). It is still a treat and shellfish is always a treat, particularly if it is local.

Halifax is about a 2 ½ hour drive from Digby. It is very attractive British-style city with its parks, flowers and gardens. It has a small town feel to it with a clean, civilized, and orderly appearance. The Titanic survivors were brought to Halifax and there is a Titanic Museum which displays many of the artifacts and historical data. A half hour drive from Halifax is Fundy's Bay and Peggy's Cove, known for 38' tides, a quaint village and hordes of tourists.

From Halifax, we drove up to Cape Breton Island toward the Cabot Trail but stopped along the way to visit the Glenora Distillery, the only distillery outside of Scotland which produces a very high-end single malt whisky. It cannot be called Scotch only because it is not distilled in Scotland. The tour takes about an hour and one does get a sample sip and the opportunity to buy a bottle direct from the distiller. It is probably cheaper in a US liquor store.

The Cabot Trail is a scenic drive around Cape Breton Highlands National Park. The views are spectacular, looking out over the Gulf of St Lawrence and the outlying islands to the west and the Atlantic Ocean to the east. The inland side looks on hills and valleys but keep your eyes on the road. It goes up and down, twists left and right, and would be a lot of fun to drive it in a sports car.

We spent two nights and a day at the Fortress of Louisburg. It was second only to Quebec as the most important stronghold and commercial city in New France in the new world and the third busiest port in North America. It protected access to the St Lawrence River for France and was the major support for the fishing industry.

It was particularly known for its huge fortifications to protect French interests and the site of a major historical battle and siege during the French and Indian War (Seven Years War). Unfortunately for Louisburg, it was a seaport that was near higher ground which made it difficult to defend. The novel *Northwest Passage* by Kenneth Roberts described the second siege in 1758 which included the exploits of Rogers Rangers and their leader, Robert Rogers. He was the original frontiersman from New Hampshire who fought against the French in the Seven Years War. Daniel Boone came long after Robert Rogers. What makes him so interesting is that many of the tactics he developed which are described in the novel are still taught in the Ranger school today.

Unfortunately, he destroyed his legacy and reputation by siding with the British during the

Revolutionary War. With all his leadership and military skills, he is not as well known in the United States as he could have been. Benedict Arnold, better known, another Revolutionary War tainted hero is the subject of other Kenneth Roberts novels, *Arundel* and *Rabble in Arms*. Kenneth Roberts seemed to write about the good side of American heroes before they went bad. Even the bad guys had some redeeming qualities. Unfortunately for their historical legacy, in American eyes, it was a reversal of the prodigal sons.

Louisburg fortifications were destroyed by the British after the siege of 1758. In 1961, the Canadian government recreated a small portion of the town as an historical tourist site. It is historically accurate and for lovers of history, a fascinating day of sightseeing.

We continued on down the road to the Alexander Graham Bell Museum in Baddeck, Nova Scotia where he had a summer home for over 30 years. The museum contains many items donated by his heirs in the mid 1950's including items from some of his inventions, boats, planes and the telephone. His interests and inventions went far beyond the telephone, and many are on display in the museum. The museum is across the bay from his summer estate, Beinn Bhreagh, where his heirs still live. There is a good sized parking lot for coaches, so we parked, left the dogs in the coach with a window partially open for ventilation and went to the museum. About an hour later, over the museum public address system came the announcement 'Will the owners of an Irish setter named Max come to the entrance lobby'. Max does not like to be left alone and he can be very resourceful. He used his nose to open the window wider, pushed open the screen, jumped out of the coach, knew where we had gone, and went to look for us. From his collar, the museum got his name. He was so proud of himself

The Caribou –Woods Island ferry is the best way to get to Prince Edward Island, the smallest Canadian Provence. The attractive campground was right across the small bay from Charlottetown. It was a nice place to sit out with a cocktail and enjoy sunset as the lights of Charlottetown came on. The next day we took the scooter to explore the island. One of the special places is the house of Lucy Maud Montgomery and the site of her novel 'Anne of Green Gables'. Then over the Stanley Bridge and the Prince

Edward Island N.P. before heading back to our campground. It did not seem like a long trip when we plotted it out, but it was 250 miles, a long drive on a motor scooter for one day even with stops. We both had saddle sores. That was our second hint, after Corpus Christi, that perhaps we should consider pulling a car.

We left Prince Edward Island via the bridge. Interestingly, taking the bridge to leave the island was cheaper than using it to go to the island, and in any case, the ferry was cheaper.

We went to Quebec through northern New Brunswick along the St Lawrence River, a casual 2 day trip. After a few weeks in a foreign country, we finally got to hear a foreign language. The campgrounds for Quebec are on the south side of the St Lawrence River and west of the bridges into the city. The Plains of Abraham, now a park, is the site of the battle that determined the future of North America and why most in North America speak English rather than French. Quebec, both the city and province, has never quite accepted that and still cherishes their French culture which makes this such an interesting city.

We did not experience the reputed rudeness of Quebec and had a wonderful time with great food, good, friendly and helpful people. It is a wonderful city to explore on foot and the old city with the city walls one of the few walled cities in North America. Quebec and Montreal are the closest thing to European cities in the English-speaking North American continent.

Chapter 4 Great Lakes

We continued on through southern Canada until we got to Sault Ste. Marie. The locks that connect Lake Superior with Lake Huron and the rest of the great lakes to adjust the 21 foot drop between the two lakes. The first lock was built in 1855 and lifted 27 ships. Now, the ship volume is over 5,000 annually. Although there are 4 locks, because of the size of the ships, only 2 are usually in operation, with a third used occasionally. Watching the locks lift or lower the giant ships is a relaxing way to spend a half hour, although the first few minutes would have been enough.

Sault Ste. Marie is very close to Mackinac Island, a definite must visit. Park the RV in the ferry parking lot, and, if you want to provide your own transportation, bring a bike or roller skates. No motorized vehicles are permitted on the island, other than some emergency vehicles. The charm of the island is that it's a community frozen in time. Hiking, biking and sitting on big front porches on wooden rockers is the primary activity. Ferry terminals are on either side of Mackinac Bridge, the bridge that connects the upper and lower peninsulas of Michigan.

The Great Lakes area of the US, sometimes derogatory referred to as 'the flyover area' usually by east or west coast 'elites', has some really neat places to visit.

The Henry Ford Museum of Transportation and Greenfield Village is Henry Ford's tribute to his idol, Thomas Edison and other business leaders who built much of the industrial strength of the country near the turn of the century. They are across the road from each other in Dearborn, MI. Henry Ford moved their homes, laboratories, or factories to Greenfield Village and created an early 1900's village filled with history. The buildings include the Wright Brothers' Bicycle Shop, a replica of Edison's Menlo Park Laboratory, Henry Ford's birth home and garage where he built the first prototype automobile. Other buildings moved here celebrated Lincoln, Luther Burbank, Noah Webster, H.J. Heinz, and Harvey Firestone. There are various events throughout the year. It is one of the best American history museums dedicated to the industrialists who built the economic engine and the industrial infrastructure of the US.

The Henry Ford Museum of Transportation has an extensive collection of antique cars and famous historical artifacts, including the Lincoln in which Kennedy was assassinated and the chair in which Lincoln was sitting when he was assassinated.

Each of these museums can easily take at least one day each to visit. I went there many years ago when in eighth grade and never forgot it.

Wisconsin Dells is a family vacation site on the Wisconsin River and Lake Delton. It is place of water slides and fudge stores. It seems like every fudge store in the country has a branch operation here. The water slides are conveniently located near the fudge stores for an enthusiastic bath for the kids.

Taliesin East, the home and studio of Frank Lloyd Wright in Spring Green, WI. There are a number of tours, one for the estate, another for one or more of the houses on the estate, and the studio and theater tour. What makes this interesting is that Wright did not expect his houses to last and they were built with that in mind. They did not have strong and what we would consider today, permanent foundations. That included his own house which has undergone extensive renovations to keep it intact. Wright's philosophy was that his houses were works of art and would, over time, disintegrate and be replaced with new works of art. He was wrong and we still enjoy many of his 'works of art'. His style was not for everyone and, because he was rather small, the ceilings on some houses were very low with narrow hallways. Wright did not want to waste artistic space on something so mundane as a hallway or walls that stretched higher than (his) eye level. Large people could get claustrophobic in some of his houses. The Kentuck Knob House described later in the section on Pennsylvania is a good example of this.

On this trip, we stopped at Algonquin campground in Algonquin, IL. The RV excursion gave us the opportunity to visit longtime friends: one of Ed's high school friends whom he hadn't seen in 30 years and a couple from our old Hartsdale NY neighborhood who moved away years ago whom we hadn't seen for about the same time.

One last visit on this trip: to see Lincoln's home in Springfield, IL. It is almost like a homage to the 16th president and to walk into his house to finally see him as a mortal. His presidency, his stature and his tragic death give him somewhat of a 'greater than life' legacy. His law office is a few blocks away and the short walk between them give one a short glimpse of his life for the 16 years he lived there.

Some of the short trips are a great break in the summer. We took a week's trip to Pennsylvania which was enough for some travel highlights.

Pennsylvania has some well-known architecture, both buildings and landscaping, two of which we visited on this trip. There is also a lot of significant military history in Pennsylvania from all the wars fought on US soil: the French and Indian War, the Revolutionary War, War of 1812, and the Civil War. The only site we did not visit in Pennsylvania was Presque Ile in Erie on Lake Erie. It was an American Naval Base for the battle of Lake Erie during the War of 1812. The actual battle was off the coast of Ohio near Sandusky.

Longwood Gardens is in Kennett Square, near Philadelphia. This estate of Pierre DuPont with over 1000 acres of gardens is one of the finest gardens in the world. It isn't very often one can hike all day and never leave the beauty and color of a garden. There is a four and half acre observatory in the garden for special plants and winter tours.

One of the great historical sites for the Revolutionary War, Valley Forge, is about a half hour drive from the gardens. For those who have limited or no knowledge of our nation's history, it is time to visit this historical site and appreciate the sacrifices and impact of these soldiers on our lives.

Gettysburg is another historical site that belongs on the bucket list for history buffs, particularly of the Civil War. With the recent TV series and movies about the war, it is fairly easy to follow the events of the battle. One portion of the battle that was very interesting and could not be seen in the panorama of the battle was Joshua Chamberlain's famous defense of the north flank of the Union defensive position on Little Round Top. This small wooded area when seen, gives a personal perspective of that famous charge by the Maine 20th. The 3-day climactic battle the beginning of the end of the Civil War. It ended the invincibility legend of Robert E Lee and demonstrated that the North had some decent commanders as well. It is about a three-hour drive from Valley Forge.

Fort Necessity was an emergency fort built by George Washington in one of the first battles of the French and Indian War, his first military engagement and his only military surrender. In 1754, the French and British were battling for trading control in the Ohio County, somewhat of a precursor for the war in North America. Washington was sent to the area by the Virginia Governor to provide protection and establish a presence for the British traders.

A battle developed under somewhat cloudy circumstances and Washington anticipating an attack quickly built a circular fort. The attack came and the French and Indian War (Seven Years War) began. Washington was forced to surrender, the fort was destroyed by the French, and Washington was sent back to Virginia by the French. The war is not well known, but was very important in the history of the United States, North America, and the world. It started the British consolidation of control over the development of the new world.

Falling Waters, the most famous Frank Lloyd Wright house is about 15 minutes away from Fort Necessity. It was built for Edgar Kaufman, a businessman who had one of the largest department stores in Pittsburgh. He was the 'Selfridge' of Pittsburgh. His son, Edgar Jr had studied under Wright briefly and from other business activities, had a relationship with FLW.

The Kaufmanns had a rural retreat at Bear Run that had a few cabins in need of repair. They asked Wright to take a look to see what he could do. He got a survey of the land, concentrating on the best site, the water fall. Kaufmann then commissioned Wright to design a new house.

A few months later, Edgar Kaufmann called Wright and said he would be in the area and would like to see the plans that afternoon. Wright had not done a thing, so he sat down and drew up the plans in a couple of hours. He did not design the house below, above, or beside the waterfall, for the view but over the waterfall, something no one envisioned. He obviously had been thinking about the design, just hadn't bothered to put it down on paper.

There has to be a message in here somewhere, perhaps some people just work better under pressure or perhaps genius knows no bounds.

Whatever it is, Wright drew up the design of his most famous house in just a couple of hours.

Wright did not always build with the long term in mind. Falling Waters did have some construction faults that required fairly extensive renovations in the 1990's. The reasons for the problems have been debated, but the artistic beauty has not been questioned.

There is another FLW house in the area, Kentuck Knob, sometimes called the Hagen house. It is the Hagen of Hagen Daz ice cream and he was a good friend of Edgar Kaufman who introduced him to FLW. His dairy farm was quite successful so he could afford to have a Frank Lloyd Wright house which was built in 1955. The house is a good example of Wright's sense of proportion – the hallways are very narrow, the ceilings are rather low and the kitchen is tiny because Wright thought the kitchen was an insignificant room not worthy of much space. The house is now owned privately by a British Lord who opens it to the public when the family is not there. Tour Tickets are only available at Falling Waters which coordinates availability with the lord when the family is absent from the house.

Chapter 5 Cross Country 1

This year, short trips were out. Maybe some visits along the way, but no more long term stays since the novelty of RV travel was waning. There were some highly rated RV parks in the Palm Spring area. I suggested to Betsy we stay in one of those parks for a month just to see what it would be like. We knew of Palm Springs and its location in the middle of a desert, but had no idea what it was like. Betsy's reaction was 'Are you out of your mind; you want to spend a month in the desert?' However, this is supposed to be an adventure, so we figured it was worth a try. Off we went for our version of a trip to 'Wally World'.

First stop, Atlanta. Evidently climate change had not yet arrived in Atlanta because it was so cold that we had to go to the local Walmart to buy an auxiliary heater. The RV furnace was not up to the task. The water hoses could not be hooked up because the water was turned off at the campground because of the temperature.

We spent a couple of nights in Vicksburg and toured the battlefield siege lines. There were limited skirmishes that occurred over a month and a half, long enough to starve the city and the Confederate troops. The position of Vicksburg on bluffs over the Mississippi River and a curve on the river that pushed it away from the town prevented the Union Navy from an assault. Its position made it akin to attacking a castle in feudal times i.e. use a siege and wait them out. Grant used his plodding but determined leadership to eventually capture Vicksburg on the same day that the Union won the battle of Gettysburg. These two victories on the same day sealed the fate of the Confederacy, but it took two more years to finally end it.

After a visit with family in Dallas, we made another trip through west Texas, pretty boring except for a stop for lunch at Abe Lincoln's Barbeque. It was at the junction of Rte. 12 and Rte. 20 just east of Van Horn, and perhaps the best BBQ we have had. Abe Lincoln said that he mail ordered his BBQ all over the country and, while we were there, was sending some to an address in Denver, CO. It could have been that it was just a welcome break from the drive through west Texas, but it was good.

A couple of days in El Paso was enough. We were put on edge just as we were hooking up in the campground when the couple on the next site asked us 'Are you packing?' Being eastern tenderfoots, we had no idea what he was talking about. He explained that El Paso is close to Juarez, Mexico and it is very dangerous and one should carry a gun. Carrying a gun into Mexico is not a good idea and our experience the previous year on the Mexican border was such that we decided to visit Mexico anyway without a gun. As in the previous year, just about everything was $3, including lunch, beer, and $3 haircuts for both of us.

We were not shot or threatened by anything other than barber razors. I guess that we did not look like potential drug customers or rich Americanos so the bad left us alone. It was far more active than the small border towns we had visited last year and a lot of fun sightseeing and shopping.

Our next port of call was Benson, AZ where hometown and RV friends of ours were part time employees/volunteers at a very nice RV campground. We spent two weeks there doing a lot of hiking in the mountains including Cochise Stronghold, the last refuge for the great Apache leader. He finally agreed to a peace treaty in 1872 and died of natural causes in 1874. It is about a 45 minute drive from Benson. It is a protected canyon with rock perches for warriors defending the camp site. When hiking through the stronghold, it is obvious why the US cavalry refused to hunt for Cochise when he was in hiding. It was a perfect place for an ambush. The Chiricahua Mountains are another great hiking area. We hiked there in January, not sure I would recommend it in July.

One of the daytrips from Benson is to Tombstone, which pretty much remains as it was in 1881. It was still the Cochise county seat until 1929. Then, rather than becoming another western ghost town, they used their historical heritage to be reborn as a tourist town. It is loaded with southwestern history, Indian wars, mining, gun fights and all the other things that made the US what it became. We toured the city and visited some museums. One of the more interesting stories was described in the Cochise County Court House Museum. A couple of entrepreneurs bought 9,000 turkeys in Mexico for $.50 each, drove them (think of a cattle drive with turkeys) 1,000 miles to San Francisco during the latter stages of the gold rush and sold them for $5.00 each. I can see a Billy Crystal movie in this.

Sierra Vista and Bisbee are also interesting towns to visit. Bisbee in particular, has an eclectic personality most of which probably came from its status as a hippy hangout in the 60's. There are excellent and diverse restaurants, art and craft shops, Victorian and other European architecture, historical and current mining sites, and ghosts. It will entertain you for the entire day and, with the ghost tours, perhaps the night as well.

Tucson is about a half hour drive from Benson toward Phoenix and the site of an annual gem exchange. This is a dealer show for gem importers displaying their wares to wholesaler distributors and jewelers. I had two cousins who sold pearls to jewelry stores, one in New England and the other on the west coast. They gave us tickets to attend which we were fortunate to get because the tickets are very limited. My cousins had influence because my female cousin is very attractive and my male cousin had a wife who was a model. Sex sells, particularly at jewelry exchanges. The show covers venues all around Tucson with pearls in one place, gems in another, jewelry and watches in yet another and others too numerous to remember. It may have been better than the New York jewelry market on 46th St because this is one of their main sources of inventory. There was lots of security, but much of it was subtler than obvious. There were the noticeable security guards, but others guards were difficult to determine whether they were customers or security personnel.

The Saguaro National Park is right outside Tucson. It is a drive-through park and is the home of the largest cacti in the nation. The giant Saguaro cactus is the symbol of the American southwest. They can be found in other areas in Arizona, but not in such a profusion. In the spring, the cacti will have flowers, which, for us easterners, can be a surprise. Also, you may see a Javelin a pig like animal, but not in the pig family. They are native to this area and feed on the cacti, spines and all.

The Biosphere is about 20 miles north of Tucson. It is a 3+ acre enclosed building, the majority of the enclosure is glass and built between 1987 and 1991. It was funded mainly by one of the Bass brothers from Texas, and intended to test whether a closed sphere could be self-sustaining. The volunteer inhabitants were expected to grow their own vegetables, maintain domestic animals and support themselves with no outside contact for 2 years. It was not successful (they cheated and evidently sent out for pizza) and is now operated for scientific research by the University of

Arizona. It was a controversial project and now, an interesting story and open for tours.

Our ultimate destination of 'Wally World' was Indio, CA, near Palm Springs for our month in the desert. When we arrived, our reaction to the desert, was 'incredible'. It was a desert dressed up in California formal attire and certainly did not have a desert feel to it. We followed our directions to Outdoor Resorts in Indio. As we turned onto Avenue 48, there was an Outdoor Resort on both sides of the street. We took a chance at the one on the left that did not have the dust and dump trucks and won. That was the one for which we had our reservations. The other was still under construction, but nonetheless was open.

Outdoor Resorts was a new experience for us. We had been in a lot of campgrounds, many of which were very nice, clean, well run, in a good location, with many activities and features. None of them had landscaping like this with an 18 hole executive golf course and 8 tennis courts all of which were available to all residents. There is a large clubhouse for community events including dinners and stage entertainment and an outdoor grill.

There were fountains, waterfalls, gardens and palm trees. And, top it off with temperatures in the 70's, humidity in the single digits, and sun all the time. No wonder people want to be here in the winter.

Outdoor Resorts became a special place for us and we knew it right away. We spent more time there than any other places we had visited which gave us the opportunity to meet lots of people. We met other 'campers' on the first day. A neighbor came over within 10 minutes to help us back into the site, then invited us over for dinner that evening to meet some other couples. It gives one an immediate sense of belonging. And there were 30 more days to go before heading home.

One of the first things we did was hop on the scooter and drive around the area. Palm Springs is on the west side of the Coachella Valley and Indio is 30 miles to the east. The valley is fairly narrow, so there are only a few east west routes, but, during the winter season, they all have lots of traffic. Palm Springs has become somewhat seedy in the past 20 years as more of the tourist business moved east with the expansion of the golf courses.

Palm Springs heyday was in the early days of the entertainment industry, beginning in the 20's. Many of the Hollywood crowd wanted a getaway, but needed to be within a few hours driving distance from Hollywood in case there was a job for which they needed to audition. During the depression, jobs were important for actors as well as for the 'ordinary folk'. Palm Springs, two hours from Hollywood, fit the bill and remained the getaway favorite and second home location. In the 50's, jet airplanes made almost anywhere close enough for an audition, so Palm Springs became less important. But the winter weather and desert beauty still kept the Coachella popular with much of the entertainment industry. Bob Hope, Frank Sinatra, Walter Annenberg and President Ford had homes there. Their estates can be seen on the local streets. Bing Crosby built an RV park still there called, (this should be easy to remember) 'Blue Skies'. Tourists can book a tour of the stars' former homes, and perhaps some current ones. It is not just for the celebrities'; the architecture is also an attraction.

Golf courses grew from 19 courses in the 60's to 138 golf courses now, mostly with lush green fairways. The growth became more dramatic in the 70's as more retirees started moving in. The golf courses were built to sell houses. New residents wanted to live on a golf course, so the developers built a golf course and then the lots for housing around it. When that phase was completed, the developers sold the golf course back to the land owners. Everybody was happy until the golf courses started to lose money. It takes a lot of golfers and water to support 138 golf courses. There may be a day of reckoning, but it doesn't appear to be happening yet.

The most interesting course and, in my opinion, the most beautiful is the Firecliff Course at the Desert Willow Golf Resort. It takes full advantage of the desert landscape with appropriate flora and fauna with desert textures and features. Not only is the landscape beautiful, the golf course is also a lot of fun to play. A couple of the holes can be seen from the access drive into the resort and a good place for lunch. Even if golf is not on the agenda, the view from the drive into the resort is worth a lunch.

George Patton and his wife spent early 1942 here as he trained his army for desert warfare in North Africa. His house where his wife lived during the war is on Avenue 48 and Jackson in Indio and the Patton Museum is at his WW II training headquarters on Chirico Summit, about 30 miles east of Indio on Rte. 10.

The Living Desert Zoo and Gardens is obviously a zoo and garden featuring desert animals and plants. But, in addition, it has one of the largest model railroad layouts in the world. The model landscape takes the trains from the desert in Palm Springs to the gold mines in the Sierras the mountains in the northwest and the Grand Canyon with places in between. It is extensive, fun and terrific for kids.

In other words, there is a lot to see and do here, too much to describe in this small book. The fun of this area is to spend time here and focus on your areas of interest.

After one month our time at Outdoor Resorts came to an end. Time to head back east. But, before we left, we made our reservations for next year, this time for three months.

This was a good opportunity to visit Death Valley. In April, it has a very comfortable temperature and if there been a steady supply of rain during the winter and the temperature is warm but not hot, the desert flowers should be in bloom in late March to early April. If these conditions are met, the desert floor is a carpet of color. It is hard to imagine how impressive the desert flowers can be. However, there is no guarantee of the right timing so check with the desert flower websites to check on the status. Even if the flowers are sparse, the geological and environmental extremes of Death Valley is unique and is worth at least a two day visit.

Next was Las Vegas, Disneyworld for adults. There is not much to say about Las Vegas that hasn't been said. It is an experience that even those of us who do not gamble can enjoy, but only in small doses – two or three days is our limit. The buffets and shows are a bit more expensive than when Las Vegas did not have any competition from casinos in Indian reservations and state authorized casinos for cheap money in lieu of tax increases. The economic law of supply and demand even works in the gambling industry, much to the surprise of state legislatures (or more so, the gullibility of the voters) who approved the casinos. There still are good deals. Best are in January, before corporate budgets are approved when there are fewer conventions and less travel resulting in less room demand and more supply.

On the return trip cross country, we were less active. But we did have an exciting experience while driving through Oklahoma. About 4:00 PM the sky was getting very dark, a storm chaser car speed past us and the sirens were wailing. We got the message. An RV in the open road is not good when tornados are in the area nor is an open campground. Destination – Walmart at the next exit. Walmart is welcoming to RVs, if local ordinances permit, and RV's frequently spend the night in a Walmart parking lot. This was one of those times, but not in their open parking lot. We parked about 5 feet from the side of the store when the storm hit. We rocked and rolled but stayed upright. The only damage we had was some flashing that came loose from the slide. Duct tape comes in very handy in these situations. It lasted until we got to an RV repair facility and got the correct screws to do the repair ourselves.

Although we were somewhat anxious to get back to see how our house survived the winter, the south in the spring is truly in its glory so we indulged ourselves. The gardens in the south are special and now are at their peak.

Natchez Mississippi is not so much a destination garden as it is a destination town. It claims to have the largest number of antebellum homes in the country, mainly because of its pre-Civil War wealth and homes and avoidance of destruction during the war. The magnolias, dogwood, rhododendron, azaleas and spring flowers are spectacular and are all through the town. The homes, restaurants and the town history, mainly before the Civil War, makes this both an informative, educational, and beautiful place to visit.

Our next stop was Callaway Gardens in Pine Mountain Georgia. It is more like a series of gardens and nature exhibits bordering the resort golf course. Some can be walked, but connecting the various gardens is best done by bicycle or driving. Individual gardens include azalea, rhododendron, and hydrangea, and the Butterfly Center.

Nearby, a 20 minute drive, is Warm Springs, Georgia and FDR's little white house. Warm Springs was originally known for its (surprise) warm springs with their health benefits which is what brought FDR here in 1924 for polio treatment. He felt that it helped him and returned here every year and eventually built the cottage that became the little white house in 1932, the only home he ever owned. From his rural experience here, he developed many of his new deal policies. He died here April 12, 1945, 26 days before the end of the war in Europe. (Also, interestingly, three days' shy of the 80th anniversary of Lincoln's death at the end of the Civil War). The house remains as it was the day Roosevelt died. There is a museum with Roosevelt mementos and artifacts, and an auditorium with a film and his two classic cars.

One of the most important, yet least known battles in the Revolutionary War, was in a small woodlands pasture used to graze cattle, called, interestingly Cowpens. It is in South Carolina, close to the North Carolina border, a four hour drive from Warm Springs, GA.

The battle is interesting for two reasons. First is the tactics of the battle and the second was the strategic impact on the war. It was one of the turning points. The operation was part of the southern campaign of the British, based in Charleston, in the later stages of the Revolutionary War. The battle was in January, 1781 and Yorktown, the final battle, was in October, 1781.

Nathanial Greene, the Patriot commander in the south, wanted to draw the British away from their supply lines in Charleston. His army was a fraction of the size of the British and he knew a direct confrontation could not succeed.

He split his forces and sent Daniel Morgan up toward western North Carolina, a very risky move but he had few choices. The British commander, Cornwallis, sent Banastre Tarleton, his cavalry commander, a much despised British military leader because of his brutality, to chase after Morgan and destroy his army, while Cornwallis would go after Nathanial Greene who stayed to the east.

The Patriot Army was made up predominately of militia, not known for its military discipline. Morgan's tactical plan was to take advantage of that reputation by drawing Tarleton's Calvary into a trap. He set up 2 skirmish lines of militia, who then scattered after firing an initial volley. Tarleton, assuming the Patriots were on the run, rushed in and faced the regular Patriot Army with their sharpshooters in place. The scattered militia who had scattered into the woods then closed in behind the British, opened up and destroyed Tarleton's Army. Out of over 900 men, only eight made in back to Charleston. The battle only lasted one hour and the main portion of the battlefield can be walked in an hour or so.

The impact of the battle forced Cornwallis to consolidate his forces and chase after Greene. That pulled him further and further away from his supply base in Charleston. He headed to Yorktown, VA to replenish his supplies from the British fleet that was sailing to that harbor. Unfortunately for Cornwallis, the French got to Yorktown first, keeping the British fleet out of the harbor. Washington and his army was able to get to Yorktown in time to trap the British, ending the war.

Brookgreen gardens, on the South Carolina coast just south of Myrtle Beach, is a garden and wildlife preserve. It is different in that, in addition to the gardens, it contains many of the sculptures of Anna Hyatt Huntington and her sister Harriet Hyatt Mayor. Both, but particularly Anna were considered among the prominent sculptors of their generation. Anna and her husband, Archer Huntington, bought the land, and opened Brookgreen as a showcase for Anna's sculptures in 1932. There are now over 1200 sculptures by 350 artists in its collection and is ranked by some organizations as one of the top ten public gardens in the country. There is not much else to say after that distinction. The azaleas here in the spring are particularly special. Of course, azaleas everywhere in the south in the spring are special but the profusion of color in the garden is what makes them so special here.

Finally, mid-April, back in Connecticut, fertilize, then mow the lawn, clean out the flower beds, trim the hedges, prune the shrubs – kind of a letdown after our travels. But summer is on its way and Connecticut is a lot better than Palm Springs at this time.

CHAPTER 6 CROSS COUNTRY 2

Driving across country for the third time was less exciting now, because the travel was no longer the most important element of the trip.

It was now time to explore the west which is where we spent most of the rest of our RV time. It was new for us and there is so much for us to see. It is also a great place for RV's because of the spectacular scenery, open space, and the National Parks.

We got to Outdoor Resorts in late December for our second season and for an extended stay this time. The lots at Outdoor Resorts are privately owned and managed and controlled by the lot owners. Many of the lots are customized by the owners with outdoor kitchens, dining, and living areas and personal landscaped areas with a shade structure over the living area. The temperature during the day is usually in the 70's or low 80's and it rarely rains. Therefore, residents spend most of their time outside and use their RV's only at night and usually just as a bedroom suite. The RV lots, fairly large by RV standards, are still close to each other. There was constant activity throughout the day, always something to see or do and never boring.

The golf course at Outdoor Resorts was short, just right for women and older folks who no longer hit the ball as they did a few years previously. It is also good for any one working on their short game. It is a pretty tough 18 hole course with water hazards on 12 of the holes. For serious long ball golfers, there are those 138 other golf courses available for a greens fee.

The resort has a very active social life, with a social director, tennis and golf tournaments and a group best ball tournament as a means of meeting new residents. Tennis was later supplemented with a new game 'Pickel Ball', a game similar to tennis somewhat like paddle tennis. Great for tennis players whose knees don't work as well as before and good exercise for those of our generation. However, Pickel Ball was not accepted with great enthusiasm by serious tennis players. They referred to it as a game whereas tennis is a sport. Seems to me to be a contrived difference. Eventually the game and the sport learned to co-exist when some of the good tennis players started playing pickle ball and enjoyed it.

As is apparent, Outdoor Resorts was designed primarily for the retired generation, both active and less active. With all the social events and common age related activities it is reminiscent of college life without the homework. The residents are from all walks of life. A few had executive positions at large companies, but most were small business owners, retired military, some doctors, lawyers, academics and a number of blue collar workers.

The common thread was that they generally were physically and/or mentally active, reasonably successful with happy marriages. A couple cannot live for months in a 400 sq. ft. home unless they are happy together.

Ages ranged from late 40's to 2 couples over 100. One of the 100 year old couples moved back into the resort after their children put them in an assisted living home. Their complaint – the people at the home were too old.

California has such a diversity of scenery that it beckons overnight or weekend side trips from the base in Indio.

Near Indio in Yucca Valley, about 20 miles away, is an old movie set called Pioneertown. It was built in 40's for western movies, including Roy Rogers, Gene Autry, Hopalong Cassidy, Lone

Ranger and many others. One of the sets, 'Pappy & Harriet's Pioneertown Palace,' is now a local tavern with notable country and well known western musicians appearing weekly. It is a popular Saturday night party event for vintage residents of Outdoor Resorts including us. Some of the popularity may be the music, but much may also be the memories of the TV westerns we watched in the 50's and tried to identify the sets from particular shows.

There are some great desert hiking trails in this area. The Mecca Hills, about 30 miles southeast of Indio has some slot canyon hikes. One, called 'the ladders' uses rustic ladders to climb up some of the canyon walls on the trail. It is about a 4.5-mile loop hike, fairly moderate, and a fun hike with many twists and turns as you maneuver through the canyon. We first went with a friend who was a geologist who described the geological environment along the trail which added to the enjoyment of the hike. He could describe and identify the colors from the various minerals in the rocks. I couldn't help thinking of what would happen in the event of an earthquake in some of the tight spots. But we were assured by our geologist companion, not to worry; there would be ample warning of one that could affect the hiking trail. There are dozens of other hiking trails in this area, some shorter, many longer. This is probably our favorite because of the distance, variation, and scenic interest.

Other hikes are in Joshua Tree National Park. The park 20 miles east of Indio is where the low Sonoran Desert on the southeast side meets the high Mohave Desert on the northwest side. The temperature and ecosystem change as the altitude changes. The hiking trails reflect the change. On the lower desert, the 'Lost Palms' hike is an easy hike of about 1 mile from the Cottonwood entrance to an oasis of fan palm trees. The difference in temperature from the hot sun to the shade of fan palms is amazing. It is not just the heat of the sun on the body, but the sun cannot penetrate the leaves to heat up the ground during the day that keeps it so cool throughout the day. There are also a number of longer hikes from this area that go up to old mining sites.

In the spring, this area has one of the best displays of desert flowers anywhere. If the weather is just right, the display is breathtaking. The local papers provide an ongoing narrative of the status of the desert flowers in various surrounding areas during the season.

On the upper desert, Barker Dam Nature Trail is easy and popular. It is a little over a mile long and scenic. Nearby is Hidden Valley Trail, an easy one mile loop to a picnic area and for wild west fans, reportedly used by cattle rustlers.

Flowers in the upper desert bloom later and, in our experience, more common to the cacti than the ground flowers of the lower desert. This is just our experience, possibly based on when we would go to see them. The cacti flowers are different, but just as colorful.

Thousand Palms is on the north side of the Coachella Valley and has a nice hike along the San Andreus Fault. In fact, you straddle it most of the hike, left foot on one side of the fault, right foot on the other. The fine stone dust on the path identifies the fault line. It leads to a fan palm grove with a little pond with flowers and shrubs. Very pretty spot for photography. There is a visitor's center there staffed by volunteers, including some that live in an onsite RV.

There are other hiking trails all over the area, including some on the mountains overlooking Palm Springs for some nice views.

Not surprisingly being on the San Andreus fault, we experienced a large earthquake on an Easter Sunday. It actually was from a different fault line than the San Andreus fault, but, since that is the one identified with Palm Springs it is automatically assumed to be the cause of any earthquake in the area. We were at a friend's house for Easter dinner and my chair started to shake. I thought Tom was behind me rocking my chair and looked around and he was in the kitchen and nobody was behind me. Then I saw the waves in the swimming pool and water slopping up over the deck. It was an earthquake that lasted about 30 seconds. For us, it was exciting because an RV in an earthquake, as opposed to a tornado or hurricane, is about the most secure place to be. It is away from tall buildings, is self-contained and is built to withstand rocking.

One year, a group of us drove our RV's into Puerto Peñasco, Mexico for Christmas. We had heard all the stories about the problems driving an RV in Mexico, but our friends had done it frequently. Puerto Peñasco is about 60 miles Southwest of Sonoyta, the Mexican entry point from Organ Pipe Cactus National Monument in Arizona and very popular with Arizonians. It was an easy trip and the RV Park in Mexico was new and very nice, right on the water. It caters a lot to the Americans since it is the closest beach for Arizonians. Therefore, the water, electricity, and roads were all up to American expectations. There are a lot of timeshares in the surrounding area filled with Americans looking for a lower cost high quality vacation spot. Seafood, particularly jumbo shrimp are a specialty and at $7/Lb., a great deal. We filled our freezers with them. Also, the fuel tanks were topped off at a third of the price in California.

Many of the residents at Outdoor Resorts also go to Mexico for prescription drugs. To fill a prescription, you had to have a current prescription for the drug including the strength and amount stated. The border patrol checks this very carefully. Once, Betsy got some prescription drugs and the border agent, new on the job and anxious to make a good impression with her boss searched Betsy and took her into the customs office, claiming that the quantity she had did not match the prescription quantity. The boss thanked her and showed her where the quantity amount was on the prescription, told her to go back to work and apologized to Betsy, told her to 'have a nice day' and said good bye. The Border Agents are very courteous and professional. They are not there to harass tourists.

Dental work is also common for Americans in the Mexican border towns. The dentists are all educated and trained via residencies in the US. The quality is excellent. The Canadians flock to Mexico for dental work which is less than half the price of Canadian prices. We had our teeth cleaned for $20. In the US it is $70 minimum. We also had a good Mexican meal, a $3 haircut and a lot of fun.

Another trip that can be a day or a week is Quartzsite. This is an event as much as a place and the ultimate honkytonk party. It is blue stones, blue collar, and blue grass all rolled into one. The site is about 15 miles into Arizona from the California border on Route 10. It is a congregation site for RV's from all over the country that come every year to camp in the desert for the winter months. It goes on for miles and has as many as 15,000 RV's at one time. The RV's just drive out onto the desert and camp. Frequently friends arrange to meet and park the RV's in a circle like a pioneer wagon train, forming a place for an evening bon fire and common cooking and play (i.e. drinking) areas. RV'ers look forward to this all year to see RV friends that may live far away during the year but to get together every winter here. It could be for a week or 2 months. About 1.5 million visitors come every year. There are RV shows, vendors, entertainment and hiking, and the original reason for its existence; looking for quartz and other minerals. There are 9 major gem, mineral and even more general swap-meets here every year during the winter season.

It is almost all dry camping but somewhat organized. Water, sewer pumps and fuel trucks make the rounds to provide necessary service since it may be difficult to wend your way out through the throng of RV's. The event used to start in January and last until the end of February, but recently RV's start arriving right after Thanksgiving and stay until the air conditioners quit in late March. Much of the camping is on US Bureau of Land Management Property and permits are readily available. This is an event that almost all RV'ers go to at least once if only for one day.

After one of the weekend trips, to Quartzsite, Steve and his wife Linda were heading back to

California. Steve is a very interesting guy with lots of interests. He builds houses, repairs electrical problems, plumbing landscaping, an award winning photographer, gourmet cook, works with fiber by spinning wool, and even knits. A man of many talents and interests. Occasionally however, he may get distracted. As he was driving along, about 15 miles down the road at the speed limit after fueling up in Arizona, he was pulled over by one of California's finest. The Highway patrolman asked Steve if had forgot anything. Steve checked his wallet, registration, driver's license, insurance card, and said 'No I think I have everything'

'What about your wife's phone'
'It should be here'

'It may be in the coach but she isn't'.

Linda was not wagging her tail when Steve returned to retrieve her.

Idlewild is a town in the mountains west of Palm Springs. It is a 45 minute drive, up the mountain to a town that looks like something from Austria. It offers a nice break from the boredom of sun and 70 degree weather every day. Because of the altitude it is much cooler than Palm Springs and, obviously very popular in the summer. In the winter, it is cool and can have snow. It is a nice place to go at Christmas time if you miss the Christmas spirit. You can play golf in the morning and go up to a hotel in Idlewild and have cocktails and dinner in front of a warm fire. There is a soup weekend where various restaurants make their soup, sell a bowl that you can carry around to the other restaurants to try their soup. In Palm Springs where the temperature in in the 70's, it just doesn't work. But, in Idlewild at 30 degrees, it is a different story

Las Vegas is a nice place to go for a weekend getaway and friends of ours, Tom and Joyce, won a free weekend there. So, off they went, checked into their hotel and went out for some food, fun and frolic, then back to hotel for the night. After a couple of nights, they headed home. They were quite surprised to have a bunch of mosquito bites but, because of the dry climate, mosquitos are not in a desert. When they got back to the RV and unpacked, they realized they weren't mosquito bites, they were bed bugs from the 'free' hotel. It took almost a week to take everything out of the RV, throw away any food, pack all their clothes in bags, and fumigate everything in the RV before they could move back in. New York and Las Vegas seemed to have the biggest problem because of the tourist activity and, evidently, are not as careful as they should be. Moral, always travel in the RV with your own bed and avoid hotels, when possible.

On another trip another friend of ours had to drive back to Arkansas by himself. His wife had flown home earlier because of a family emergency. Wives are very important when traveling in an RV and not just because of beauty and companionship. They fulfill an important role, like, checking up whether the driver does things completely and correctly. Jerry stopped for fuel, filled up the tank, and was on his way. A policeman waved him down and asked him if he normally drove an RV with a tail hanging out. Since Liz was not there to keep track of everything, Jerry had driven off with the fuel nozzle, hose included still in the fuel tank. He could laugh about it much later, but at the time, it was a rather expensive oversight.

We shared many RV stories with other RV'ers, one of our favorites came from some Canadian friends. Years earlier, they just bought their first RV, a 25' camper. When they had to empty the black water tank, they were a bit too far from the drain pipe and their hose could not reach it. But, they came prepared and had an extension hose. So Jack told Judy to hold the 2 hoses together while he opened the valve. Judy and Jack are very good looking and Judy was immaculate in her personal appearance. She never went out without makeup and beautifully dressed. And because Judy loved Jack and they were happily married, Judy did what Jack asked.

The black water is semi solid and comes out with a lot of force, and while most Canadian women are strong, they are not that strong. The way to connect an extension to a black water hose is to use a hardware connector rather than a two hand manual connector. What you probably can picture is exactly what happened. This is the ultimate demonstration of a happy marriage because they are still married.

There are lots of driving experiences that are funny in hindsight, but not so much at the time. Ray, a Canadian friend had just picked up his new RV and was driving down to Indio. He was going down a narrow, canyon road with a lot of twists and turns. As he took the first left curve, the right slides in the RV started to open. He then had a right hand curve and the right slide went back in and the left slide opened. The road was quite narrow with canyon walls on both sides and no place to pull over. He managed to get to the bottom of the road with everything intact so the problem then became, 'how do I get this back to the dealer'. He was a pretty good engineer, so he drove carefully, slowly and with very strong bungee cords, and with the standard strong Canadian wife to help hold the slides in, he made it back to the dealer who then put in the hydraulic fluid they forgot to add to the slide out system. As we all learn over time, Trust but Verify.

PART 2 NINE YEARS OF RV LIVING

CHAPTER 7 FULL TIMING

We had considered buying a lot at Outdoor Resorts after the first year, but wondered if it would really be as nice the second year. We rented, we liked, and we bought. For us, the advantage of buying was to be able to customize our site environment as one would do for a home, be able to come and go on our own schedule and to be part of a community. We got involved with the social life and became active members of the community.

However, one must be aware, even though it is an RV resort, it is a gated community in California, just chock full of type A personalities. But, of course, not everyone is Type A. There are a lot of B's and C's and we had friends in all groups.

As the season came to a close in mid-April, the question of living full time in an RV came up. As empty nesters, a big house in Connecticut no longer made sense. So we knew we were going to move somewhere, but where. Our youngest daughter, Sara was in New York City, the older, MaryBeth in Seattle Washington. We had spent time with Sara because of our proximity to New York. MaryBeth, on the other hand, was far away and we hadn't been able to see her as often. It was time to spend some time with her. The RV would give us some flexibility, but it is best to have a residential anchor somewhere. The RV is a wonderful portable home without permanence and the perfect solution during our transition from empty nest to a permanent home. But even a portable home needs a community for a feeling of stability. Outdoor Resort became our residential anchor for the winter.

However, there was a logistical problem; what do we do with the furniture in the house if we live full time in an RV. One thought was to put it into storage until we decided to move back to a house. Another idea was to rent out the house furnished while we lived in the RV. None of those ideas was appealing to us.

Then, we found that the windshield in the RV was popping out and we had to leave it for the summer at the factory in Oregon for repairs. That solved a problem with the logistics of making the move. Since our family Thanksgiving was in Tenafly NJ this year, there was no reason to leave Connecticut until then. So, we had until

Thanksgiving to pack everything we wanted to keep in a 6' X 12' trailer. We could then tow the trailer across the country to our daughter's house. To finish off the closing of the house, we had a tag sale to sell what we could and the rest went to an auctioneer.

An additional consideration for this plan is that our next door neighbor owned the local United Van Line franchise and when we considered storing the furniture, he showed us that it was far better to sell and buy rather than store and move. Besides, we had no idea where we would eventually move or if our furniture would be appropriate for the house we would eventually buy. The decision then became easy – we put the house on the market and started packing.

Cleaning out the house and packing up the trailer was difficult, kind of like the experience of families heading west on the Oregon Trail and packing up all their possessions in a Prairie Schooner. We had one more problem. We had 6000 pounds of stuff packed into a 3000 pound capacity trailer. It took 3 flat tires on the trailer along the way to give us the hint that we had a problem. By then, it was too late and we were committed.

Leaving in early December, pulling an overweight trailer, and taking the northern route was kind of risky. But, defying all common sense, that is what we did. We were very lucky: it snowed behind us in the all places we just left. The only time we ran into snow was just as we arrived in Seattle and the car and trailer slid down Marybeth's driveway.

We picked up the repaired RV in Oregon and continued on to Indio for the winter in our new lot at Outdoor Resorts. Most of our friends had already arrived and the social season began and continued until mid-April. We interrupted our fun in the desert and drove the car up to Seattle to share Christmas with MaryBeth, then brought the trailer down to Indio for storage. It became our mobile basement for anything that did not fit into the RV, mainly books.

Chapter 8 California, Oregon

Spring is the start of the travel season when Outdoor Resorts winds down after the winter season. In late March, residents start leaving and by the end of April, the place is almost deserted. This was the first year we were not going back to Connecticut so we needed plans for the next eight months. Certainly, travel is nice, but eight months of constant travel is a bit much. We wanted a summer residential anchor as well. Friends in Indio owned a site in a small RV campground in an old fishing camp on the Siuslaw River in Florence Oregon called 'Coast Marina'. They invited us up to join them for a couple of weeks. So we made our travel plans to head up to Florence, Oregon.

We took Rte. 395, on the eastern side of the Sierra Nevada, a more relaxed drive north than Rte. 5 on the western side. There are a number of interesting historical sites along the way.

Lone Pine is a small town in the Owens Valley, that, because of its scenic and geographically interesting terrain, became a popular location for filming western movies starting in the 1920's, and continuing on to today. The main movie set was the Alabama Hills, on the west side of the town. The original incentive for the movie set was its scenery and the access to Los Angeles. Into the 1950's, that was still an incentive but the scenery and the infrastructure that had been built up over the years and the low filming cost kept the movie industry busy here including many movies other than westerns.

Lone Pine is an access point to Mt Whitney the tallest mountain in the lower 48 states and the southern termination of the John Muir Trail that starts in the Yosemite Valley. We were there to pick up our daughter, MaryBeth who had just finished the hike after 22 days.

Manzanar, one of the Japanese detention centers during WW II was located here and some of the Manzanar buildings remaining are part of the Manzanar National Historic Site Interpretive Center. It is the best known and best preserved of the detention camps. The center has a significant collections of photos, drawings, painting, and artifacts associated with the camp. It shows how the internees adapted and made the best of a bad situation by decorating their accommodations, planting gardens and starting small businesses to survive. Other buildings were sold off when the camp was closed and some are still used as residences in Lone Pine.

About 150 miles north of Lone Pine is SR 270 that takes you up a mountain road, some of which is dirt, to Bodie, CA, a true ghost town at an altitude of almost 8500 ft. Bodie was settled in 1859 when a small cache of gold was discovered there. At about the same time, the Comstock Lode was discovered in Virginia City, Nevada which boomed while Bodie just survived. Bodie finally started their boom era in 1876 when a profitable deposit of gold was discovered. Two years later, a larger vein was discovered and Bodie became a mining boom town. The saloons, bordellos, and mines lasted for about 10 years. However, there was still enough mining left to support a small mining business, so boom excesses were replaced by churches and families. The last mine closed in 1942 and the town was deserted and it now is an official ghost town. It is maintained in a state of 'arrested decay' which means it is not being preserved but still protected by the state from vandalism. There are over 100 building still standing, just as they were left. In the houses, there is old furniture and old and peeling wall paper on the walls. The commercial buildings still are stocked with goods left when the residents left in 1942. It is a very dry climate which has reduced the rate of decay of the buildings. It is fun to walk the empty streets and imagine life in the boom time.

About 100 miles north and a 2-hour drive is Virginia City, the site of the Comstock Lode which is not quite as high as Bodie at 6150 ft. Virginia City was also founded in 1859, about the same as Bodie, but it boomed immediately. The Comstock Lode was not part of the California gold rush, 10 years earlier, but it was just as significant. At that time, gold and silver had the same monetary value. In many ways, Virginia City followed a similar time line as Bodie. It started earlier, but slowed down around the same time, in the 1880's. However, Virginia City was much bigger and survived longer. It has a bit more history to it, partially because of the start of Samuel Clemons writing career first as a reporter for the local newspaper then as writer, Mark Twain. Virginia City has a colorful past and, unlike Bodie, has been preserved and now has a successful tourist economy. There are good western museums and musical and theatrical entertainment as well as the walking around a historical town which creates some authentic looking history.

As we continue north toward our Oregon destination, a nice overnight stop is Reno. It is much lower key than Las Vegas but still entertaining.

Coast Marina in Florence Oregon is the exact opposite of Outdoor Resort. It is rustic in a laid back small community on the Oregon Coast. Very restful after the hustle and bustle of the California desert social life. Instead of 400 sites, there were 40. Social life was in the clubhouse usually for a community dinner.

The Oregon Coast is spectacular and the dogs loved to run along the beach. However, it is not a good swimming beach without a wet suit. It is cold, but the winds make it very popular for wind surfers and para surfing. Florence is a quaint small town with great sea food. It is on the Oregon Sand Dunes which is rather unique. The golf courses are Links courses even though one of them, and my favorite, Ocean Dunes is about 8 miles inland from the coast. It was built on the Florence Dunes which gave it much of its Links style. Each hole is different, with its own character and golf shot options. Only a couple of holes are parallel and they on a separate nine.

One of the real benefits of Florence is the summer weather. It rarely gets over 80 degrees and is usually dry, just about perfect. Florence is also known for its rhododendrons which grow in abundance, and the largest concentration of black bears in Oregon. Hiking is more popular than wind surfing.

Coast Marina seemed like a good option for our summer residential anchor, but we wanted to check out some other options. So we headed north to visit our daughter north of Seattle. The scenic route was along Rte. 101 on the Oregon coast.

Driving along the Oregon coast is a picture postcard at each turn. The coast line, the fishing villages, and the gardens make it a photographer's dream. The drive north along Rte. 101 to Astoria takes about 4 hours, past the Tillamook Cheese plant.

Fort Clatsop, Lewis and Clark's winter camp in 1805 is in Astoria. It is a replica of the original cabin. The winter that year (and most winters) was miserable with constant rain, high winds and limited food sources. The elk, which had been a major source of protein, knew about winter weather and left for higher ground. The Indians were willing to trade, but the expedition had nothing the Indians wanted. As good as fish is to eat, one needs a break once in a while. It was a tough winter and even though many got sick, they all survived and were looking forward to leaving. They never got to enjoy the glorious summer weather.

Chapter 9 Western Canada

After a few days with Marybeth and a day trip to the San Juan Islands, we drove to Canada for an extended trip. We spent some time with two of our best friends from Indio, Ray and Maxine who lived in W Vancouver. Ray was a very successful businessman who was very proud that he succeeded even though he claims he barely graduated from high school. He was dyslexic, stuttered, heavy and smart as a whip. He is as good a story teller as anyone I have ever known, charming with an advanced sense of humor.

He enjoyed toys and has a lot of them, one of which is a 62 ft. yacht. One weekend a friend of his was visiting and suggested they go out on his 'boat' for the weekend. He would cover the fuel cost. 'Great idea' said Ray. While fueling up, the attendant yelled to Ray, 'Do you want me to fill it up or stop at $3000?' His friend went pale and mumbled, 'Maybe we should just go out for an hour or so.' Even though we are good friends, I never volunteered to pay for the fuel and we never took a cruise.

Ray drove us around Vancouver then up to Whistler Mountain where the Winter Olympics were to be held the following winter. As we were admiring the beauty of the area, Ray reminded us this was the summer. There is a reason why they go to Indio in the winter. Rain gets very monotonous after the 6th month.

We took the ferry boat to Vancouver Island and the capital, Victoria. If you make reservations early, (like at least 6 months early) you may get a reservation at West Bay Marine Village., and possibility one with a view. It is the most popular RV Park in Victoria because of the location, right on the bay where the ships enter the harbor and a view across the water to the skyline and lights on Victoria. It is also a nice, two mile walk along the water to downtown. Victoria is a beautiful and walkable city. It is the capital of BC with the Parliament buildings. There are parks, flower gardens and peddle taxis for transportation in the town.

Flower baskets are hung from the street lights and the store fronts are well maintained and welcoming. The Empress Hotel is one of the grand old elegant hotels and, if nothing else, walk in and look around. If you feel flush and wish to enjoy British tradition which is still popular here, have high tea. It is an experience for those that can afford it.

About 11 miles north is Butchart Gardens, one of the great gardens of the world. The climate along the coast of BC is a gardener's paradise and Butchart Gardens takes advantage of it. The gardens were originally a limestone quarry which is the source of the money used to develop them. When the limestone supply was exhausted, Mrs. Butchart decided to do something with the empty pit. Starting in the early 1900's, the sunken garden was developed. It became a popular tourist site in the 1920's and has been expanded over the years to its current status. There is good public transportation to the gardens from Victoria and is easier than driving.

Tofino is a fishing village on the western coast of Vancouver Island just north of the Pacific Rim National Park. It is a rustic fishing village with a very rugged beach and a popular vacation spot, particularly for nature lovers and whale watchers. Some Canadian friends who live on the island say that they love to come here on a stormy weekend to watch the storms, their version of July 4 fireworks. The storms can be very dramatic and intense. On those weekends, they drive their car and rent a house with a view of the ocean. Not the right time and place for RV's. To get there from Victoria, drive north about 95 miles to Qualicum Beach and take Hwy 4 west about 80 miles to the coast.

Back to the mainland and a drive to Lake Louise in Banff National Park, Alberta, Canada to meet some friends from Connecticut. Lake Louise is two and a half miles west of the town of Banff which is very pretty, very crowded and very expensive. We stayed a couple of nights in the campground at Lake Louise while we visited with our friends then headed north to Jasper.

The road from Banff to Jasper is known as Icefields Parkway because the mountain ice field feeds eight major glaciers. One of them, the Columbia Glacier, can be seen from the road and explored by a hiking trail or via a glacier snow coach available at the visitor center. The Columbia Glacier has been receding since 1847 long before global warming became fashionable when there were not as many humans breathing out CO_2 nor cars burning fossil fuels. Not sure how to evaluate this, but these are just the facts.

Banff is dressed more like 'business casual', not formal, but still a bit upscale. Jasper is strictly 'shorts and sneakers'. They both have great scenery and hiking trails. In Banff, we camped in a neat campground and took a nice trail around the lake. In Jasper, a herd of elk was roaming around among the RV's and the hike went down along a river with waterfalls and lots of mosquitoes. It probably had to do with the trail we took which had some still water and high humidity that day, but they were so thick, only a shotgun would put a dent in the mass.

Edmonton is a 4-hour drive east. It is a large city with a population of close to a million. The first megamall was built here in 1981 and expanded 3 times since then. Other malls have been built since then that are larger, but the West Edmonton Mall was the original. One can enjoy a water park, see a hockey game, go shopping and never leave the mall.

Our personal highlight of this trip was the Calgary Stampede. This is ten-day party and Calgary goes all out for it. It is a combination of county fair, community breakfasts, and nonstop B-B-Q. The primary attraction is the rodeo. It is an international event hosted by Calgary and they do it with hospitality and class.

The opening events of each day include pancake breakfasts held at various sites all over the city. They are hosted by community organizations, corporations, shopping malls and anyone else who decides to host one. There are dozens every morning and all draw big crowds. Bar-Q-Ques are now gaining popularity with community organizations but there is a lot of competition with the local bars and restaurants who are packed with customers.

Stampede parties, both public and private have a reputation of somewhat frisky behavior with the consumption of large quantities of alcoholic beverages. The Stampede is the Mardi Gras of the north without any pretensions of religious values.

The opening day festivities start with a western orientated parade. There are the usual bands, floats and community organization marchers, but also hundreds of horses, rodeo participants and First Nation Indian Dancers.

The rodeo is one of the largest, richest payout, and probably the most famous rodeo in the world. It draws the best and toughest rodeo competitors in the world. The competition includes men and women, experts and young up and coming novices. The evening event after the rodeo events is a stage show by 'The Young Canadians' a popular entertainment troupe, originally a grandstand act just for the Stampede but now popular all over the world, including Olympic Games and the Tournament of Roses Parade. They put on a great show.

We had one of our nicest experiences while riding the train from our campground to Stampede Park. Two young boys, about 14 or 15, that live 50 miles away in the country, introduced themselves to us, wanted to know where we were from and told us all about the Stampede and Calgary. They were so impressive and polite to us, and enthusiastic about their city; it set a tone for our entire stay and left us with such a warm feeling.

We were told about Drumheller by a number of Canadian friends. It is about 50 miles east of Calgary and is part of the badlands with the erosion and interesting hills and hoodoos associated with badlands. It is sometimes referred to as the dinosaur capital because of its rich history of dinosaur bone discoveries there. The Royal Tyrrell Museum of Paleontology is perhaps the premier dinosaur museum in the world, and certainly one of the best museums for the exhibit presentations we have ever seen. The dinosaur exhibit is a chronological presentation of dinosaurs from the earliest to the last. It demonstrates the progression of the dinosaur age visually and puts it all in perspective. There are also exhibits of prehistoric plants and marine reptiles. It is an extraordinary museum.

The other feature here is the golf course. It is unique. The front nine is the original 9-hole standard golf course. Years later the golf course got the rights to a section of the badlands that bordered the original course. It was developed for the back nine and very different from the front nine because of the badlands terrain. Almost all of the drives are over gullies and require precise aim and distance. One requires a 200+ yard carry. That was a problem for some of us older golfers who left their long drives behind when we turned 70. But it is a fun course to play and to remember. Just be sure to bring extra (and ready to lose) golf balls.

After Drumheller, came a drive to 'Heads Bashed In' buffalo jump. This was how early Indians tribes harvested buffalo. Prior to the introduction of the horse and large scale hunting, a buffalo jump was set up to stampede buffalo over a cliff to their deaths. They would then harvest the remains. It was a fairly common practice throughout the western plains. However, in the US, the bones from the jumps were all taken for the calcium and used in much of the building of the west. Luckily the US did not have access to the Canadian sites so this one has been preserved and is now a UNESCO World Heritage Site. The visitor's center has a nice museum that describes the process with some archaeological artifacts. It is near Fort MacLeod, about 50 miles north of the Montana border, near Glacier NP.

Since we were so close, this was an opportunity to visit Glacier National Park. It eventually became our favorite summer campsite. We knew there was a famous 'Road to the Sun', but there was so much fog and rain, we could not see anything. But we would eventually see a lot of it.

We drove on to Coeur d'Alene, Idaho to visit Betsy's cousin who has a summer house on the lake. Just another beautiful place with green mountains meeting the deep blue lake and on the northern shore, an attractive resort with the special golf course with a floating island green. The only one I have ever seen that requires a small yacht to take the player from the tee to the green and, obviously, the return trip. We watched the golfers playing it from the restaurant. It is a resort golf course, so it is expensive, but with a unique hole. I have no knowledge about the other holes, having never played the course.

A high school friend of Ed's was an orthopedic surgeon in Yakima, WA. This was a good opportunity to renew an old friendship from high school and college days. It had been years other than Christmas Cards, since we had been in contact. Again, we took advantage of the RV lifestyle to get in touch and visit friends from years ago.

We then headed back to Seattle to spend some time with our daughter. After a few days there, it was on to Portland to visit more friends from Connecticut and a cousin not seen in many years. Finally, back to Florence to buy a lot in Coast Marina. Nice to have a summer site as well as a winter site. Still a month or so to settle in to our new summer home.

While in Florence, I joined the Elks Club after being told of their extensive Elk's Club RV Campgrounds, most in the west. It is one of their major fundraisers for the charities they support. Members of the Elks have access to their RV Campgrounds at a very reasonable rate, usually $20 or less. Many have full hookups, or water and electrical with a dump station. Some may only provide parking sites for overnight stops. The Elks Clubs in the Napa Valley were particularly nice. There were also other good locations as well. The Elks Club in San Jose was right across the street from the CalTran commuter station train to San Francisco. It is the most convenient and least expensive campground in the San Francisco area. The club in Oakhurst, CA is the closest campground to the south entrance of Yosemite NP. It did not take much urging for us to join, especially Betsy, because they usually have a good restaurant with reasonable prices.

On October 9, the rain starts and doesn't stop until May 15. Time to leave Florence but Indio is still in summer and the temperature is over 90 degrees. Outdoor Resorts is still empty. Now the fall travel season.

Chapter 10 Rocky Mountains

We had about a month and a half to travel on our way down to Indio, CA. Our neighbors in Indio owned a RV park, Rocky Mountain RV Park in Gardner, MT at the north gate of Yellowstone NP. We met friends from Indio for a preseason social gathering before we would all see each other again in a couple of months in Indio. It is always enjoyable to visit Yellowstone. It so large that there is always something new to see and do. There are enough books about Yellowstone that nothing we can write will add anything new.

A three-hour drive from Yellowstone is Cody, Wyoming, named after Buffalo Bill, where he lived for many years. The Buffalo Bill Museum in Cody is a great American history museum and probably the best western history museum. It is now affiliated with the Smithsonian. It is five museums in one. The primary one is the Buffalo Bill Museum an exhibit of his life and times including his Wild West Show that made him so famous and the image of our western history throughout the world. Others are the Plains Indian Museum, Whitney Western Art Museum, Cody

Firearms Museum and the Draper Natural History Museum.

The Plains Indians are the Arapaho, Lakota (Sioux), Crow, Cheyenne, Blackfeet and Pawnee. The museum displays artifacts and information about their history, traditions and culture. The Whitney Western Art Museum has original western paintings and sculptures by Frederick Remington and other western artists. Another famous western artist, Charles Russell has a museum in Great Falls, MT. The Cody Firearms Museum is the most complete collection of American firearms in the world as well as firearms from world manufacturers and shows the evolution of the technology to current day. The Draper Natural History Museum has animal specimens with displays of the geology and environment of the area. There is too much here to absorb in one day. Leave something for a return trip.

There are two routes from Gardiner, MT to Cody. The easiest is to take Rte. 89 through the north gate of Yellowstone, to Rte. 14 which takes you to the east gate and onto Cody. If you are in an RV, this is the best route. However, if by car, one of the great drives is via Rte. 212 (Beartooth

Highway) through Coulter Pass to Rte. 296 (Chief Joseph Highway) to Cody. The distance and time is about the same and both have nice scenery, but the Chief Joseph Highway is one of the great and historic drives. However, it takes a lot of switchbacks to go through the valley. The valley route means that there are switchbacks going into the valley and switchbacks leaving the valley. It is the route Chief Joseph took in eluding the US Calvary as he led his followers to Canada. He missed by 40 miles, but his retreat became one of the great examples of leadership under adversity.

From Cody, it is about 200 miles and a little over 3 hours to the Crow Agency, the Little Bighorn Battlefield National Monument. It is operated by the Crow Indians who were scouts for Custer, some of whom were killed in the battle. Most, however were with companies not involved in the battle.

The battle of the Little Big Horn was fairly short and very decisive. However, there are many opinions about the details of the battle, i.e. where and how Custer was killed, who killed him, who died first, etc. That is for historians and archeologists to debate, but the battle itself can be visualized from the Last Stand Hill (more like a knoll). From the parking area, (RV parking is available), the Last Stand Hill is in front with a monument and fence around the site. From there, one can see the ravine with gravestones showing where the soldiers fell. There is also a four and a half mile self-guided driving tour of the park that describes the troop movements prior to and after the battle. By combining the driving tour with the walking trails in the ravine, one can get a pretty good picture of the activities of that fateful day.

The drive to Colorado Springs is a relaxing day drive and if you are not in a hurry, Cheyenne is a good place to stop and take an hour drive around town. An interesting western history footnote, on Rte. 25 on the way to Colorado Springs, about 150 miles south of Crow Agency, is the town of Kaycee. About 40 miles west of Kaycee on county and dirt roads is the 'Hole-in-the-Hole' or 'Robbers Roost', Butch Cassidy's hideout. It is popular with back packers not RV'ers because of the condition of the roads. The rugged country makes it clear why it was chosen as a rustler/robber hideout.

We spent a couple of days in Colorado Springs. It was on the way we were heading and it has some interesting places to visit. Probably the most well-known is the Air Force Academy, about 15 miles north of the city. It is a very large campus which isn't too surprising because of the need for airplane runways, parachute landing areas, glider training, and everything else related to the air force. Since it is the newest of the military academies, it is more modern than traditional campuses. The chapel is the most striking and photographed building on the campus. When we visited, we took the tour and then watched new cadets taking their first parachute jumps and the training for glider pilots. The visit is obviously more than just looking at buildings and watching cadets marching.

We went to the Broadmoor Inn for lunch. It is well known by ice skating fans for the Ice Skating competition, but the resort is well known by fans of luxury living. It was built in 1918, and modeled after the finest European resort hotels, the landscaping was designed by Frederick Law Olmsted, the landscape architect of Central Park in New York, the first golf course was designed by Donald Ross, a second course by Robert Trent Jones and the shooting school was run by Annie

Oakley. The resort was first class from the beginning and has remained so to the present. We have been to a few 5 star resorts, but only for lunch. So we get to see it, enjoy the food, some of the amenities and leave with our wallet still intact. The Broadmoor lunch was reasonable and the visit was worth the lunch.

The next day, we visited the Olympic Training Center. It is a large complex, 35 acres, located conveniently near downtown Colorado Springs. If you want to meet some Olympic athletes close up and personal, this is the place to go. The athletes are easy to identify because they are the only ones that are fit. The facilities include an Aquatic Center for swimming and water polo events, two Sports Centers each with 6 gymnasiums, Fencing and Pantheon Center, Shooting Center and a Velodrome for biking events. In addition, there is a Sports Medicine Center for all sorts of diagnostic, training and treatment facilities. There are also the living facilities including the athletes dining facilities. The center also hosts various events throughout the year including some international competitions.

Our final visit was to the 'Garden of the Gods' so named because someone years ago thought that the rock formations had the makings for a beer garden. It consists of red rock formations in all sorts of shapes – some slanted, some straight up, some toppled, all made by glacial upheaval and erosion. It has some of the characteristics of the red rock formations in Utah and Arizona, but different in that it borders the Colorado Mountains and the beginnings of the desert plains, associated with Utah and Arizona. It is a popular hiking, mountain biking and rock climbing recreational area for residents and visitors. There are good roads through the park with good parking areas to get out and walk. We hiked around in the park and, because of the rock formations, could pretty much stay in the shade. The formations are dramatic and fun to see up close as we walked around.

The road to Pikes Peak, Rte. 24, is close to the Garden of the Gods but we did not bother to do it. We have driven up many mountains and the toll of $25 was not worth it to us but may be to others.

Next stop, Durango, CO. Durango is, first of all, a pretty small town and, secondly, the center of some interesting places to visit. The

Durango/Silverton Narrow Gauge Railroad starts its 90-mile trip to Silverton here. It has been in operation since being built to carry silver ore down to Durango in 1882. Now it carries tourists along one of the great scenic and historic trips in the west.

However, rather than take the train, four of us drove the mountain road which parallels the train route. The scenery was the same, and the historical narrative came from the brochure we read along the way. Both routes take about an hour for the 50-mile trip, but the drive gave us a bit more freedom for lunch and exploring the town. Also, since there were four of us, it was cheaper driving and gave us a bigger budget for lunch.

Mesa Verde is about 45 miles west of Durango. It has the largest best preserved archeological sites of the Ancestral Pueblo natives and their cliff dwellings and therefore one of the best parks to see Southwestern history.

The plateau was known for a number of years, but the cliff dwellings tucked below the plateau surface were never seen until 1888 when they were spotted by some cattle ranchers, the Wetherills, after being told of them by some natives. They invited a Finnish archeologist to examine the ruins. After he took some of the artifacts back to Finland for further study, the site was put under federal protection.

The Cliff Palace is the most famous and largest of the cliff dwellings and is available for a fee tour. The others, Balcony House, Spruce Tree House and Wetherill Mesa Long House and Step House also require tour tickets. I am somewhat fearful of heights and The Balcony House has a series of ladders that, by themselves, are not a problem, but together, seeing that the base of the top ladder was close to the edge of a 3000 foot drop to the valley, was a bit nerve-wracking. MaryBeth who joined us for this trip and climbs mountains, thought nothing of the ladder and just scooted right up.

The cliff house tours are necessary to appreciate them. There is some accessibility for wide rim wheel chairs for The Spruce Tree House and the Step House and an overlook for the Cliff Palace. Hiking on the plateau leads to more exhibits and some nice exercise, and possibly a picnic.

Mesa Verde is one of the most interesting places we visited. There are other cliff houses, Montezuma's Castle off of Rt 17 in Arizona and

Canyon de Chelly, also in Arizona, for example, but neither is as extensive as Mesa Verde.

Goulding's Trading Post and Lodge is the commercial center of Monument Valley, and two and a half hours west of Mesa Verde. This is the beginning of some of the most spectacular scenery in the world. Over 30 movies have been filmed here, not all of them westerns. John Ford made 12 movies and John Wayne appeared in five movies shot here. The house that John Wayne stayed in while filming some of his movies is the old potato cellar for the trading post. The Trading Post has a nice campground centrally located to tour the valley.

From Monument Valley, you can loop through, alongside, and around the spectacular scenery that makes Utah such a destination for tourists and especially RV'ers. Drive north on Rte. 163 and Rte. 161, to Moab, which takes you along the eastern edge of the Red Rock country. Moab is an outdoor adventurer's paradise – white water rafting, 4 wheeling in the desert, mountain biking, horseback riding and hiking can keep most adventurers occupied for weeks. And the scenery is pretty nice also. We did a three-day rafting trip down the Colorado River through Cataract

Canyon with a return flight over Canyonlands National Park. The rafting was exciting, food great, tent accommodations fine, even with a little rain, and the swim in Lake Powell was refreshing. The flight back was unforgettable if you do not get airsick like Betsy.

We have returned here a few times, with other friends who like to 4 wheel in the surrounding area. This is a unique place for all the outdoor activities available to visitors.

Continuing on north is Arches National Park that can be driven and hiked. Continue the loop via Rte. 70 and Rte. 89 to Bryce Canyon. Zion Canyon is about 120 miles further southwest. These are nice parks for hiking and are quite different. Bryce is kind of like a miniature Grand Canyon in that you hike down into the canyon and into a hoodoo jungle. Zion, on the other hand, has characteristics closer to Yosemite with hikes that go up from the valley floor. I particularly like the hikes in Zion behind the waterfalls. Zion also has some nice slot canyons with streams which are fun as long as it is not raining with the threat of a flash flood.

This area is so well known there is not much to say that can't be found in other guide books. But be mindful when hiking to take lots of water and remember, in Bryce Canyon, the altitude is 9,000+ feet. That altitude will affect your respiratory system so you may get short of breath. Zion is a little over 3,000 feet, not as much of a problem.

From here, it is little over 2 hours to the north rim of the Grand Canyon. It is not as spectacular as the south rim; - it is steeper so there is only one place to look down to see the Colorado River. But there are more trees in the campground so it is cooler. When we were there, we saw a huge bird about 30 yards from us on a rocky ledge. It was a condor and with binoculars we could see the tag '138', the 138th bird released from the breeding sanctuary in California. A number of eagles, not liking the competition for the food supply, started swarming around and attacking the condor. It took off and it was an impressive sight to see it spread its 9-foot wing span. The eagles were like song birds compared to the size of the Condor.

Back to Indio for the winter by way of Las Vegas.

Chapter 11 Southwest

Spring has arrived in Indio and it is time for us to leave. We have been to Arizona a number of times while driving coast to coast, but this time, we wanted to see some places we had missed.

One of the places friends told us about was a golf course in Parker, AZ, on the border of California, called 'Emerald Canyon Golf Course'. We went at the beginning of May, before it got too hot and after the snow birds left so we could get a good tee time. Also, although not planned this way, summer green fees, $30. Even the seasonal fees are not excessive; Winter, $60, Fall, $45, Spring, $40. This is now called 'The Jewel of the Desert' and it has earned the title. The course is, by definition, a canyon golf course, with some holes driving into the canyon, some out of a canyon, driving on top of a canyon, driving to the bottom of a canyon and all things in between. The views are terrific, probably 11 of the 18 holes could be considered signature holes.

The 17th hole is quite interesting. It is a par 5 for men because there is a long fairway, a drive and one good fairway iron, to a layup area, and, if done correctly, puts your ball right to the top of a bluff, next to the ladies' tee which, for them, is a par 3. If a ball goes out of bounds, leave it. There are rattlesnakes in those areas.

There is an RV camp ground right across the road. Very convenient. We now stop here for a round of golf every time we come through this area.

In Phoenix, it is spring training for baseball. There are 15 major league teams that train in the Phoenix area all in the Cactus league. It starts in mid-February through the end of March. Friends of ours have a winter home in Phoenix and volunteer at the ball parks and give retrieved foul balls to their grandchildren.

Taliesin, Frank Lloyd Wright's winter home and studio, is in Scottsdale, a Phoenix suburb. It is a complementary home and studio to Taliesin East in Spring Green, Wisconsin. He came to this area in the mid 1930's and moved here for the winter in 1937. The environmental contrast from the Wisconsin agricultural green landscape to the Arizona desert sandy landscape stirred his imagination. Wright has always taken advantage of local building materials and Arizona had rocks and sand. Very different from Wisconsin. He used those materials to develop his own style of desert architecture. His home and studio is open to the public and remains the winter home of his FLW School of Architecture and the headquarters of the Frank Lloyd Wright Foundation.

Sedona is a red rock bonanza. Everything is red rock to the extent that, if you are not used to it, you can get overwhelmed by it and long for something green. Sedona is a short detour off Rte. 17 from Phoenix to Flagstaff. From Sedona to Flagstaff, Rte. 189 goes through Oak canyon, a beautiful drive.

From Flagstaff, it is about a four-hour drive to Canyon de Chelly in the Navajo Indian Reservation. The campground in the park is dry camping next to the visitor's center and close to the drive into the canyon.

The visitor's center has a cafeteria that is reasonably priced and has good food, with lamb their specialty. Since we both like lamb, this was a real treat for us.

Tickets for the tours into the canyon are sold here. The canyon is still occupied by Navajo families who live predominately off the land and practice their traditional culture and religious ceremonies. They give tours into their canyon on old Korean War army trucks that are rugged enough to take you through streams, over dirt paths through underbrush and anything else in their way. It is an interesting tour both for the route, but also the Navaho narrative that goes with it. There are a number of cliff dwellings here, but, are more singular, rather than the communal living of Mesa Verde. A second tour is the overlook around the top of the canyon. Seeing it from above, after driving through it below, is a different and interesting perspective.

Chaco canyon, yet another Anasazi ruin is 4-hour drive from Canyon de Chelly. This is a different type of settlement. It's an archeological site not an occupied community. It was a Hopi and Pueblo Indian community with pueblo buildings more so than cliff dwellings. It has the largest concentration of ancient ruins north of Mexico. The largest, Pueblo Bonito had over 650 rooms and was 4 stories high and built with some sophisticated architecture for the time.

The archeological research has been going on since the mid 1800's and continues to this day. The park is managed by the National Park Service and the surrounding area by the Bureau of Land management.

Back to civilization by driving through the mountains and local roads to Rte. 25 and Albuquerque. It is a nice city. Its main attraction is in the fall with the balloon festival, the largest balloon festival in the world. Supposedly, Albuquerque has a unique wind pattern because of the surrounding mountains that cause the winds to move in a horizontal box pattern, so that balloons rise, then travel west, drop to a lower altitude and travel back east, toward the launching site. This may be the theory, but the balloons and the wind have a mind of their own so chase cars are still used. Spectators can also be participants by helping with launches and descents. If lucky, you can ride in one of the balloons as ballast. It is a very colorful festival during both day and night.

We went in a caravan with 14 other coaches and had purchased tickets made a year earlier for front row sites overlooking the launch site. It seems that when we got there, someone with a lot of influence took over our sites. Our tour leaders went to find out what was going on and protest our treatment. They went to the headquarters that had news reporters, film crews and other media milling around. In comes our leaders, one on crutches from polio he contracted when he was five. The other was a very nice, but large commanding Jewish lawyer from New York. Media people love these stories. The meeting lasted 5 minutes and within 45 minutes we were on the front row overlooking the launch site.

Our leader, Kim Pollock uses crutches as a result of childhood polio. We took a trip with him and his wife to China. When we went to the Great Wall, the Chinese told him, apologetically, that they did not think he would be able to walk along the top of the wall. He replied 'No problem' and took off on his crutches so fast they just stared at him as he sped to the top of the mile long grade.

Santa Fe an hour northeast is a special city. Not large, population is only 70,000, but with extensive southwestern culture, particularly the restaurants, art galleries mainly along Canyon Road and, of course, the Santa Fe Opera in the summer and the Aspen Santa Fe Ballet. It is a walkable city with many art and history museums. Historically it is the oldest state capitol in the US and the terminus of the Santa Fe Trail.

Seventy miles north is Taos, another arts center. The sun and air here seem to work well with artists. They claim that it makes colors more vivid. It must be true because a lot of world renowned artists have studios here. Also, the Taos Pueblo is a mile north of town. It is very large, and the oldest continuously occupied buildings in the US, with about 150 residents and native enterprises. To me, it was like a living Chaco Canyon.

When the Spanish expedition of Coronado came here in 1540 looking for the seven cities of gold, they saw the adobe buildings with straw in the adobe walls. The reflection of the sun on the walls looked like gold and they initially thought they found one of the seven cities. At least, that is the story. I never saw that in a history book, but then, that is reason to actually go to see and listen to the stories for yourself.

Chapter 12 Glacier NP

We had been spending most of our summers at Coast Marina, in Florence, OR. One day, talking to a neighbor, he mentioned that he had volunteered at Glacier National Park the previous year. That is something Betsy and I had wanted to do, but the opportunities were limited and the demand is high. The stack of applications is so large, that there is no way the park staff can review all of them. Probably the best way to increase your chances is to have a personal contact. We got a name and Glacier NP was added to our travel agenda that summer. So we made a personal visit, met the contact ranger and introduced ourselves. It also happened that the park had a problem in one of their campgrounds and needed someone to start ASAP. We were in the right place at the right time. Our contact, Angie was one of the reasons there were very few opportunities – she was so well liked that no one ever wanted to leave and returned every year.

After that month in Glacier, we put our site in Coast Marina up for sale and spent the next three summers as volunteer campground hosts at Glacier NP. We would have stayed longer, but by then it was getting time to give up our nomadic lifestyle.

Glacier has west and east side administration units. They have different characteristics; the west side is more family oriented with access to tourist activities like water slides right outside the park with more stores and motels; the east side is rustic, backwoods, and wilderness, more for the hardcore hiker and photographer. Both sides have wonderful scenery and hiking trails. We were on the rustic east side, which, in our opinion, has the best campgrounds

Going to the Sun Road is the signature feature of the park. It was built on the side of the mountains and connects the east and west sides via Logan

Pass. The west side of the pass has the distinctive scary character of the road with sheer drop offs, twisting and narrow sections and spectacular views. The east side, is less scary, not nearly as many twists and turns and fewer sheer drop offs. When repairing the road, this is the route for any of the large trucks. It still has beautiful views and requires careful driving. As scary as the road appears to visitors, more bicyclers are killed on the road than visitors in cars. Rarely does a car have a problem that could cause an accident. But, if a brake fails on a bicycle as they go down the mountain, there are limited options.

Many Glacier is the most popular campground on the east side. It has a hiking advantage because many of the hikes start right at the campground. The Many Glacier Lodge, is rated the second best of all the NPS lodges with spectacular views of the lake, a mountain background and a view of the remnants of the Grinnell Glacier. Only the Ahwahnee Hotel in Yosemite was rated marginally higher, mainly because of the food. We had good friends who were the campground hosts at 'Many Glacier'. They had stories of campers waiting at the entrance for campers to leave, then racing other campers for the open site. Tom and Faye had a lot of experience and patience and were able to keep things under control. We did some hiking with them, but Tom had been in the US Forest Service and was in good shape. They would leave us far behind.

Most of our time was spent in St Mary's Campground at the east end of the 'Road to the Sun'. It is one of the larger CG and the only one, at least while we were there, on the east side with a cell phone signal. There just happened to be a Verizon Tower on the mountain with a direct line to the camp ground. For volunteer hosts, that was a distinct advantage.

We also spent time at 'Two Medicine' campground to the south and close to East Glacier, MT, the East Glacier Hotel and train depot. In my opinion, it is the prettiest campground; it is the only campground right on a lake with the mountains behind it as a backdrop. The mountains have some nice hiking trails and mountain goats in the lower section and mountain sheep in the higher section.

In the spring, moose may be in the lake and a herd of Elk may be seen wandering around the campground. We had friends from Indio visiting us one spring and on their last day said they were disappointed that they had not seen a moose. We told them to look outside and there were two moose grazing right outside their RV.

Two Medicine also has Ranger talks in the evenings about the geology, animals, Glacier history and the wilderness landscape. One ranger has a very effective dramatic background and a good sense of humor. His presentations are always entertaining, for kids and parents and brings that humor with him on ranger hikes he leads. On one of his hikes, he talks about scat and how it is used to track and identify animals. At one point on the trail, he points out some and says that it looks like moose scat. He goes over to check it out and appears to pick up a piece and takes a bite and confirms that it is moose and female and continues on. He had substituted an M&M chocolate piece for the scat.

St Mary campground gets the most activity. One summer, a small group of campers from Calgary got a little carried away with the freedom permitted in our park compared to Canadian Parks. In Canada, no drinking is permitted in parks. Here, wine and beer is permitted in moderation with the assumption that moderation should not have to be defined. About midnight on a Friday night, two women came to the door of the RV and said that there were some campers running through the campground, swearing loudly and disturbing the other campers. Betsy said she could handle it and went to the campsite. Four males were drunk as skunks and a female girlfriend was trying to settle them down. She seemed to be getting things under control. We had been through this before and were able to take care of the situation. Betsy came back and went to bed.

A half hour later, the women returned so this time, we both went over. We used the park service radio access and called law enforcement. Two law enforcement rangers were there in about five minutes. After about 15 minutes of discussion, two more rangers were called and one of the campers with some persuasion was put in the ranger car. One of his friends said that he wanted to go with his buddy and proceeded to urinate on Betsy's shoes. He got him his wish to join his buddy and off they went and things quieted down in the campground.

Two of the rangers took the culprits to Kalispell to be weekend guests at the county detention center. As they were on the way over the 'Road to the Sun' at 2 AM, a camper complained that he was going to be sick.

One of the rangers was a small feisty woman from Texas, turned around to him and snarled, 'you do and you will be cleaning up with your tongue!' A meek 'yes ma'am' and things quieted down except for buddy number 2 saying 'I don't think this was such good idea.'

On Monday morning, they went before the judge and were fined $500 each, payable in cash, wire transfer, bank check in US funds. Then came their next problem; Canadian holiday, all banks closed. So another night as guests of the county. Finally, on Tuesday, their friends drove down from Calgary with the bank checks and took the prisoners back home. It was the only real conflict in three years at Glacier, and in the end, is just a good story.

One late spring day, a man came into St Mary on a bicycle and set up a camp site in the most open area in St Marys. I only mention that because it was still snowing even though it was mid-June. The next morning when we were making our rounds, there he was, snug in his sleeping bag in a tent that had collapsed under the weight of the snow. We invited him over to warm up with some hot coffee or tea. He was an interesting person, in his early 60's and was biking from Voyageurs National Park, Minnesota, where he had been the head ranger, to Whitefish, MT for his son's wedding. So far, he had biked 1,100 miles and still had 70 miles to go to Whitefish, assuming he took the 'Road to the Sun'. He was then planning to continue on to Oregon then return and be back in Minnesota by fall. At 30, I would love to be in that kind of shape but at 60, I can't even imagine it.

In the opposite situation, a group of former high school friends from Minnesota came to the park for a post high school reunion. They were nice kids and having a good time when they decided to take a short hike up to a beaver dam. It is a three mile hike and fairly flat. But there is a fork at the half way point and if you turn right, you come back to the campground. If you turn left, it is a 7.5 mile one way hike. It is a nice hike if you are prepared for it with great views of St Mary Lake. They started around 5 PM and wore shorts and flip flops. Furthermore, the clouds were assembling for a strong mountain storm. This was not a good combination. However, being young and looking for adventure, at the fork, they turned left. They were getting cold and it was getting darker and harder to see the trail. Two guys took off in one direction looking for the trail and got lost. Then they all got lost and went off course. But, the good news was that they had their cell phones and in St Marys, they could get a cell phone signal. The bad news was; they could not tell the rangers where they were.

After a lot of searching and shouting all were eventually found by 11 PM and brought back to the campground, wet, cold and hungry. We invited them into the RV and between their dry clothes and what we could provide, they got warmed up, their clothes washed and dried and fed with some hot clam chowder. And now an adventure they can share with their kids.

The only criticism came from one of the park ranger from Minnesota who was embarrassed that school kids from Minnesota did not know better than to hike in flop flops.

We had an extended Chinese family scheduled to stay for a week. There were 15 in the family and they used two campsites. Normally the rules restrict any site to a maximum of four campers. They just about doubled that limit. But they were not causing any harm, so we could be flexible. On the second day, however, they strung up their clothes lines and hung out their laundry over both camp sites. With the amount of laundry hung out, it appeared that they were operating a Chinese laundry. Somehow, that did not seem fitting for a national park. We suggested that they take their laundry somewhere else. They had no problem since it was already dry and they were leaving the next day anyway.

There are some rules in the park where there is little flexibility. One which is strictly enforced is not to drive any vehicle longer than 28' beyond the Rising Sun campground about eight miles from the entry gate on the 'Road to the Sun'. One couple with a 36' class A, and a motorcycle on a lift in the back ignored the warnings. Some people are born stupid and some are just arrogantly stupid. With a 36' RV, it had to be the latter. They drove almost 15 miles before they were stopped by park rangers. Now, the problem was that there was not a good place to turn the coach around. Siyeh Pass, a very sharp turn ahead, is the end of the wide road and tight even for the legal work trucks. The RV driver had to back out for about five miles, causing lots of traffic problems for other visitors and a lot of embarrassment and a fine.

One of the highlights of our time in Glacier was the Blackfoot Nation Rendezvous in 2009. It was a four-day meeting and celebration of the four tribes of the Blackfoot Nation. The only Blackfoot tribe in the US is in Browning, MT, bordering the east side of Glacier. The other 3 tribes are in Canada called the First Nation. The Rendezvous 2009 was held in St Mary, next to the Visitor Center right in our front yard, a fascinating experience for anyone who enjoys history. The local tribe set up their ceremonial circle and organized the tipi (tepee) area for visiting tribes, including Crow and Sioux who joined in the festivities. Fun trivia: I learned at the Rendezvous from a Crow woman; Blackfoot Tipis use 4 poles as the tipi base and the other plains Indians, Crow and Sioux use three poles. Now you know.

The festivities started with a parade of each tribe in all the regalia, headdresses and traditional ceremonial clothing into the Rendezvous area with great dignity. There were dances for all sorts of occasions within the circle. Watching the activities and listening to the drums, makes it seem we were back in the 1870's. The Blackfoot Indians are known historically as warriors and traditionally not particularly friendly to the white man. However, during their circle ceremonies, many of the men discussed their service during WW II, Korean War, and Vietnam War. They took great pride in their service, mostly in the Marine Corp. They still have that warrior culture.

There still remains resentment with some Blackfeet Indians who feel that Glacier NP should be theirs, but most are friendly and work in the park. In Browning, there is a good Blackfeet Museum staffed by Blackfeet natives. It is not large, but very well done and presents their history with natives there to explain the exhibits and answer questions. There is also a museum store for native crafts. The Blackfeet also put on native shows and dances in all campgrounds on the east side, usually once a week.

Browning is also the main shopping area for groceries for volunteers in the east park. It has the closest supermarkets and it is pretty good. If not Browning, we had to go to Canada for groceries and that meant checking with customs to see what could be brought into the USA and what would be confiscated. At one time, we could not bring anything containing lamb, including dog food. Who would have thought that was a problem? Other than the problems with customs, the grocery markets in Canada were good.

Most visitors to Glacier NP are there to hike and we were the same. We enjoy hiking and could tell campers about many of paths we had taken. We took the shorter hikes, seven miles or less for two reasons: first, we needed to spend time in the campground to assume our responsibilities and second, we don't have the energy for longer hikes. (The first reason is an excuse, the second is true). Also, I have fear of heights, so some hikes went beyond my comfort level. In particular, the Highline Trail from Logan Pass goes along a narrow mountain ledge with a cable attached to the mountain wall as support and a 100 The building of the Bunker was done in secret and kept that way until 1992 when the site was no longer needed because ICBM's made it obsolete.

 foot drop on the other side. It is especially popular for guys trying to impress their girlfriends, or vice versa.

Perhaps the most popular hike at Many Glacier is 'Iceburg Lake', a 10 mile round trip with an elevation gain of 1200' much of which is the first quarter mile, fortunately when your legs are still fresh. The trail leads through snow fields, to a mountain lake that has icebergs even into August. That may be when it is most likely to be closed because it is very popular with bears who are getting ready for hibernation by gorging themselves with huckleberries along this trail. There are a lot of huckleberries in Glacier. Interesting trivia that satisfied my curiosity; huckleberries have a dimple, blue berries have a crown. Also there is a difference in size and sweetness.

St Marys has nice hikes some requiring the use of the shuttle bus or a car to get to the trailhead. Virginia Falls, which includes St Mary Falls is one of the most popular hikes. It can be extended to three water falls, St Mary Falls, Virginia Falls and Baring Falls. Virginia Falls is one of the prettiest falls in the park. It can be seen in the distance from Rte. 89 as you climb the hill after leaving St Marys and looking off to the right. The Glacier shuttle is a convenient way to access this trail head because after hiking past Baring Falls, you end up on the Road to the Sun and can take the shuttle back to your campground or car.

Avalanche Lakes is a popular day hike in the Lake McDonald area. It is a little over 2 miles each way ending up at Avalanche Lake. This trail may have bears just coming out of hibernation and looking for food so it could be closed to hikers. Bear food consists of roots and bulbs, not humans, but don't assume that they will turn down any food. Therefore, do not leave any food along the trail. They may look at that as the appetizer and you as the entrée. Also, as the name suggests, this is an avalanche path during spring thaw.

From Logan Pass, the Highline is popular but too high for me. It has a relaxing hike, Hidden Lake Overlook. It leaves from the Logan Pass Visitors Center, the high point of the park and close to the tree line so is open with wind and sun. Besides the views, there is a good chance to see wild life, at least mountain goats and possibly bighorn sheep. You can continue on for another mile and an elevation drop of 500 ft. to the lake itself.

Two Medicine, like Many Glacier has most of the hiking trailheads at the campground. One that we would take friends on was Aster Falls, and per our normal distance hiking, a mile and half each way. It leads to a cascading water fall. On the way, there are beaver ponds and possible moose sightings. At the end, there is a fairly steep climb of 500 feet to a beautiful view and overlook of the lake.

Goat Haunt on the Canadian border is a long, 6 miles each way hike to Kootenai Lake. The trailhead is at the ranger station on the border and, if you come via Canada, you will need a passport. There is a ranger there that checks them. The lake is the most likely place to see moose. Betsy went off in front of us on a hike to take a picture. When she came back a few minutes later, we looked back and two moose were right where she had stood.

Chapter 13 Shenandoah NP

It was time to bring our eleven-year adventure to a close. We had been looking for a place to settle down and, as much as we loved the west, we are easterners at heart. We were brought up and lived all of our lives in the east and most of our family was there. We talked to Angie, the Glacier Park ranger for whom we volunteered and asked about a volunteer opportunity in an eastern national park. She checked around and found us a place in Shenandoah NP in Virginia. That was perfect. It was the area we were interested in for our search.

Shenandoah is the weekend national park for suburban Washington DC, Baltimore and Philadelphia. Also, Charlottesville and Richmond, VA. There are a lot of people who like to camp in this area, and some are not quite ready for it.

A newlywed couple from Washington DC came to the campground on their bikes. They were young, idealistic and incredibly naïve. They planned a six month journey biking across the country on their honeymoon and Shenandoah was their first stop. They set up their campsite and put up their tent, started the campfire and got ready for the night. About 10 PM, we had a knock on the door. The young wife was upset and very frightened. 'There is a bear near our tent. Can we sleep in the RV?' We went out to see what was going on. There, up a tree, was a bear cub, more frightened than the young couple. We cautioned them to be sure to put all their food in a bear box next to their site and the cub would go away. He was just looking for food. That was not good enough so we let them sleep in our car. They left the next morning. We have often wondered just how far they got on their adventure. Certainly, Glacier NP would be a challenge.

Because of its accessibility from the eastern population centers, Shenandoah was far busier than Glacier. Campgrounds were always full on weekends in nice weather and almost full in marginal weather. We did a number of hikes, including one to Herbert Hoover's fishing camp in Shenandoah right next to a trout stream. It was his equivalent of Camp David and, after falling into disrepair, has been restored. Although Glacier had more and longer hiking trails, the hikes in Shenandoah are steeper and, for their length, more strenuous. The altitude is lower, but the humidity is higher so the effect on your body is somewhat similar. In the west we puff more, in the east we sweat more.

Our campground was near Charlottesville and the presidential homes of Jefferson, Monroe and Madison.

We had been to Monticello and Ash Lawn, Monroe's home. But Madison's home only 30 miles northeast of Charlottesville, in Orange, VA was privately owned and not open to tourists. In 1983, it was given by the homeowners to the National Trust and a Montpelier trust was set up to restore it and open it to the public. The outside of the house was restored to the 1820 appearance by 2008. Archeologists continue to work on the grounds while restorers are working on the inside and giving tours to the public. The tour addresses both projects so you can watch the archeologists still digging in the grounds and restorers working on the inside. It is a plantation house, not quite as magnificent as Monticello, but more so then Ash Lawn which is more of a farm house.

The Shenandoah Valley was very active during the Civil War. Winchester was the site of many skirmishes. New Market Battlefield right off Rte. 81, 20 miles north of Harrisonburg is remembered because the Confederate Army recruited cadets from 2 military schools in the valley and defeated the Union Army in 1864. There is a state operated Civil War Museum at the Visitor's Center for the Battlefield. It is an excellent museum.

We took a day trip to Greenbrier and the Homestead to see Sammy Snead's golf courses. He was the head pro at both places and was known for charging $50 for golf tips if you greeted him. Not sure if that is true, but there are a lot of similar stories from the locals and guests at the resorts. Once he was playing a round of golf with the head of Goodyear Tire and had a side bet for a set of tires. Snead won and Goodyear sent him four tires. He responded very simply, 'a set is five'.

The Greenbrier is also known for the 'Bunker', a cold war emergency government site built in case of a nuclear attack. It was conceived and developed during the Eisenhower administration and completed in 1961. The Greenbrier was chosen for a number of reasons, and golf was not one of them. It was shielded from nuclear fallout by the mountains surrounding it and was about 7 hours from Washington, the amount of time in the 1960's to get to a safe area in the event of a nuclear attack. Also there was good train service since it was originally built by the railroads as a resort destination. The road limitation was solved by building Rte.64 and a landing strip was added for large jets. (The cover reason was 'corporate use')

The construction was done under the guise of an addition to the Greenbrier for corporate conventions. It was a convincing story because much of the resort was and still is used for conventions. No one seemed to notice that there was a 25 ton door flush against the wall leading in to the main convention center room. It could be closed in seconds and withstand a bomb blast. Nor were the two lecture halls, the smaller one had a 100 person capacity and the larger had seating for 435 ever questioned. But, behind a door in the main room marked 'Danger, High Voltage' were dormitories for over 1,000 people with a hospital, pharmacy, medical lab, communication center, and a large power plant and water tanks. It was amazing how it was kept a secret for so long. It was only put on notice once, in the Kennedy administration for the Cuban Missile Crisis.

The building of the Bunker was done in secret and its existence was kept that way until 1992 when the site was no longer needed when ICBM's made it obsolete.

They now give tours and history buffs, architects, and the curious will enjoy the tour. With the separate power plant, it is perfect facility and is now used for date storage and computer back up facilities.

An hour and half drive northwest of the Greenbrier near Fayetteville on Rte. 19 is the New River Bridge spanning the New River Gorge. You may not recognize the name, but you probably have seen it many times in advertisements. This is where they bungee jump off the bridge into the gorge, 875 feet below. When you drive over the bridge, it doesn't seem much more than driving over any very high bridge. However, there is a visitor's center and a road that takes you down the gorge and under the bridge so you can see the engineering that supports the bridge.

No pedestrians are allowed on the bridge except for one day every year in October, 'Bridge Day'. That is when it is closed to vehicular traffic and open only for foot traffic. It is the day for daredevils to jump off the bridge. They recommend using a tethered bungee cord, B.A.S.E. parachute, rappelling, or a highline zip line, but anything else other than suicide attempts seem to be allowed. This is a big event with a lot of food vendors and day long blue grass music. People look forward to this all year and come from throughout the country to watch, film, and (maybe) participate.

Heading from south west on Rte. 19 from the New River Bridge in Fayetteville, WV about 20 miles is Beckley and Tamarack, the 'Best of West Virginia Artisan Retail Center. It is a showcase of the best West Virginia crafts set up originally by Sharon Percy Rockefeller to demonstrate the extraordinary craftsmanship of West Virginia artists, fabric, woodwork, pottery, and glass blowing among other talents. It is a great place for special gifts and Appalachian treasures. In addition, the cafeteria is operated by the Greenbrier Culinary School. It is about half the price of a meal at the Greenbrier.

Our Thanksgiving reunion was in Hilton Head this year. After Thanksgiving, we headed cross country again.

Chapter 14 Final Trip

This was our final adventure. We went back to California that fall to sell our RV and lot.

However, before we sold them, we had one last celebration. It was our turn to host the family Thanksgiving reunion. Since most of the immediate family, other than MaryBeth, lived on the east coast, the nieces and nephews would not be able to join us in Indio, CA. We decided to modify the Thanksgiving tradition and invite our west coast cousins. So, with sisters, brothers in law, both daughters, Sara and MaryBeth and cousins, 34 of us celebrated the Dingledy Thanksgiving in the desert.

Betsy organized Thanksgiving for friends and family out of our RV. Since these are long weekend event, plans included breakfasts and a Mexican dinner on Friday evening.

It worked because of our outdoor kitchen and dining facilities and the additional facilities of neighbors. Also, we cooked most of the meal on Tuesday and everything was cleaned up that night. Thanksgiving dinner was taken out of the refrigerator, heated up and laid out. We ate on picnic tables set up on the edge of the golf course.

The only problem we had was the easterners' misconception of the desert weather in the winter. Day times are wonderful, sunny with temperatures in the 70's. However, at night, temperatures are often in the 40's. Ed's sisters and brothers in law packed for daytime temperatures. They froze in the and there is only so much room in a warm RV, certainly not enough for 34 guests. Luckily, we knew where all the local thrift stores were to get some inexpensive ski jackets.

That spring, we sold the RV and our lot to a couple looking for their adventure. If they have as much fun as us, they are in for a good time.

We are easterners at heart and most of our families are in the east. Now for our trip back there without the RV, only our 6X12 trailer from the trip west ten years earlier.

An interesting trip – perhaps the basis for another story for the future.

While volunteering in Shenandoah, we had time to explore places for our next experience in life and chose the Asheville, NC area. It had what we wanted, mild winters, temperate summers, long springs and falls, Brevard Music festival and the beer capital of the east.

We miss the RV, Outdoor Resorts and Glacier, but this is now our home and we have settled in to our new life adventure.

Made in the USA
Middletown, DE
20 December 2015